OPPOSING VIEWPOINTS® SERIES

I08I0831

Animal Rights

Other Books of Related Interest

Opposing Viewpoints Series

The Future of Food
Genetic Engineering and Gene Therapy
Green Politics
Hunting and Conservation

At Issue Series

Ethical Pet Ownership
Invasive Species
What Should We Eat?

Current Controversies Series

Agriculture
Climate Change and Biodiversity
The Industrial Food Complex

> "Congress shall make no law ... abridging the freedom of speech, or of the press."
>
> *First Amendment to the U.S. Constitution*

The basic foundation of our democracy is the First Amendment guarantee of freedom of expression. The Opposing Viewpoints series is dedicated to the concept of this basic freedom and the idea that it is more important to practice it than to enshrine it.

OPPOSING VIEWPOINTS® SERIES

Animal Rights

Avery Elizabeth Hurt, Book Editor

GREENHAVEN PUBLISHING

Published in 2025 by Greenhaven Publishing, LLC
2544 Clinton Street,
Buffalo NY 14224

First Edition

Articles in Greenhaven Publishing anthologies are often edited for length to meet page requirements. In addition, original titles of these works are changed to clearly present the main thesis and to explicitly indicate the author's opinion. Every effort is made to ensure that Greenhaven Publishing accurately reflects the original intent of the authors. Every effort has been made to trace the owners of the copyrighted material.

Cover image: Andyborodaty/iStockphoto.com

Cataloging-in-Publication Data

Names: Hurt, Avery Elizabeth, editor.
Title: Animal rights / edited by Avery Elizabeth Hurt.
Description: First edition. | New York : Greenhaven Publishing,
2026. | Series: Opposing viewpoints | Includes index.
Identifiers: ISBN 9781534510135 (pbk.) | ISBN 9781534510142 (library bound)
Subjects: LCSH: Animal rights. | Human-animal relationships. | Animal welfare.
Classification: LCC HV4708.A556 2026 | DDC 179.3--dc23

Manufactured in the United States of America

Website: http://greenhavenpublishing.com

Contents

Chapter 3: Which Kinds of Nonhuman Animals Should Have Rights?

Chapter 4: What Would Be the Consequences if We Afforded Rights to Nonhuman Animals?

The Importance of Opposing Viewpoints

Perhaps every generation experiences a period in time in which the populace seems especially polarized, starkly divided on the important issues of the day and gravitating toward the far ends of the political spectrum and away from a consensus-facilitating middle ground. The world that today's students are growing up in and that they will soon enter into as active and engaged citizens is deeply fragmented in just this way. Issues relating to terrorism, immigration, women's rights, minority rights, race relations, health care, taxation, wealth and poverty, the environment, policing, military intervention, the proper role of government—in some ways, perennial issues that are freshly and uniquely urgent and vital with each new generation—are currently roiling the world.

If we are to foster a knowledgeable, responsible, active, and engaged citizenry among today's youth, we must provide them with the intellectual, interpretive, and critical-thinking tools and experience necessary to make sense of the world around them and of the all-important debates and arguments that inform it. After all, the outcome of these debates will in large measure determine the future course, prospects, and outcomes of the world and its peoples, particularly its youth. If they are to become successful members of society and productive and informed citizens, students need to learn how to evaluate the strengths and weaknesses of someone else's arguments, how to sift fact from opinion and fallacy, and how to test the relative merits and validity of their own opinions against the known facts and the best possible available information. The landmark series Opposing Viewpoints has been providing students with just such critical-thinking skills and exposure to the debates surrounding society's most urgent contemporary issues for many years, and it continues to serve this essential role with undiminished commitment, care, and rigor.

The key to the series's success in achieving its goal of sharpening students' critical-thinking and analytic skills resides in its title—

Opposing Viewpoints. In every intriguing, compelling, and engaging volume of this series, readers are presented with the widest possible spectrum of distinct viewpoints, expert opinions, and informed argumentation and commentary, supplied by some of today's leading academics, thinkers, analysts, politicians, policy makers, economists, activists, change agents, and advocates. Every opinion and argument anthologized here is presented objectively and accorded respect. There is no editorializing in any introductory text or in the arrangement and order of the pieces. No piece is included as a "straw man," an easy ideological target for cheap point-scoring. As wide and inclusive a range of viewpoints as possible is offered, with no privileging of one particular political ideology or cultural perspective over another. It is left to each individual reader to evaluate the relative merits of each argument—as he or she sees it, and with the use of ever-growing critical-thinking skills—and grapple with his or her own assumptions, beliefs, and perspectives to determine how convincing or successful any given argument is and how the reader's own stance on the issue may be modified or altered in response to it.

This process is facilitated and supported by volume, chapter, and selection introductions that provide readers with the essential context they need to begin engaging with the spotlighted issues, with the debates surrounding them, and with their own perhaps shifting or nascent opinions on them. In addition, guided reading and discussion questions encourage readers to determine the authors' point of view and purpose, interrogate and analyze the various arguments and their rhetoric and structure, evaluate the arguments' strengths and weaknesses, test their claims against available facts and evidence, judge the validity of the reasoning, and bring into clearer, sharper focus the reader's own beliefs and conclusions and how they may differ from or align with those in the collection or those of their classmates.

Research has shown that reading comprehension skills improve dramatically when students are provided with compelling, intriguing, and relevant "discussable" texts. The subject matter of these collections could not be more compelling, intriguing, or urgently relevant to today's students and the world they are poised to inherit. The anthologized articles and the reading and discussion questions that are included with them also provide the basis for stimulating, lively, and passionate classroom debates. Students who are compelled to anticipate objections to their own argument and identify the flaws in those of an opponent read more carefully, think more critically, and steep themselves in relevant context, facts, and information more thoroughly. In short, using discussable text of the kind provided by every single volume in the Opposing Viewpoints series encourages close reading, facilitates reading comprehension, fosters research, strengthens critical thinking, and greatly enlivens and energizes classroom discussion and participation. The entire learning process is deepened, extended, and strengthened.

For all of these reasons, Opposing Viewpoints continues to be exactly the right resource at exactly the right time—when we most need to provide readers with the critical-thinking tools and skills that will not only serve them well in school but also in their careers and their daily lives as decision-making family members, community members, and citizens. This series encourages respectful engagement with and analysis of opposing viewpoints and fosters a resulting increase in the strength and rigor of one's own opinions and stances. As such, it helps make readers "future ready," and that readiness will pay rich dividends for the readers themselves, for the citizenry, for our society, and for the world at large.

Introduction

> *Science has made enormous progress in the last 30 years. It's clear that animals are not brute beasts; they have complicated forms of perception, some of which humans don't even have.*
>
> — *Martha Nussbaum*

In the seventeenth century, philosopher René Descartes wrote that animals are nothing more than complex machines, or *automata*, as he put it. They have no feelings, no experiences. They are no more conscious than is your bicycle or your watch. Descartes defended his position by saying that this view, "is not so much cruel to beasts but respectful to human beings … whom it absolves from any suspicion of crime whenever they kill or eat animals."

Not everyone at the time agreed with Descartes, of course. But while most people at that time clearly saw there was a difference between a cow and a watch, the idea of offering legal protections—rights—to nonhuman animals was held by only a few. Things have changed quite a lot over the centuries. Today virtually no one would agree with Descartes' position, even if it did remove some twinges of guilt. In fact, a growing number of people feel that animals have the right to at least some protections. A 2022 Gallup poll found that almost half of Americans believed that existing animal cruelty laws should be strengthened. The same year, an online poll of Canadians found that they, too, are increasingly supportive of animal rights. As of 2025, roughly six percent of the US population and a similar number in Western Europe follow a vegetarian diet. Four percent are vegan, meaning they don't eat or use any animal products at all.

However, the issue of animal rights is complicated. Acknowledging that animals have feelings is one thing. Granting them rights is quite another. Any discussion about animal rights must grapple with some difficult questions: What's the difference between animal welfare and animal rights? Exactly what rights should be accorded to animals? And perhaps most vexing of all, to what animals should we extend rights? Should we include animals we eat? Should we include insects? The viewpoints included in this volume address those questions and more.

The first chapter starts with a look at the current state of animal rights around the world and offers some background on the history of the animal rights movement. You may be surprised to learn how various countries approach the issue and what laws are already in place.

In the second chapter, the authors dig in to the main question: Do nonhuman animals have rights? In order to answer that question, we have to determine if they are conscious, if they can feel pain, and if they do feel pain, does that mean they are actually suffering? All of these questions are trickier than they might seem, and involve a lot of scientific and philosophical work. The writers here are doing that work.

When most people think of animal rights, they think of farm animals, pets, animals used for research, and charismatic wild mammals, such as whales and polar bears. However, only three percent of animals are vertebrates, or animals with a backbone. When we talk about animal rights, should we be talking about the rights of lobsters, jellyfish, roaches, and spiders? The authors in the third chapter take on this difficult question.

The final chapter explores an issue that is often skimmed over in discussions about animal rights: What are the likely consequences of granting rights to *all* animals? Would we be able to nourish ourselves? Would we be able to produce new medicines? Would the environment be improved—or might it be damaged?

These days, virtually no one thinks animals are machines, and people increasingly believe we should treat them better. If we are going to do that, we need to carefully consider many difficult questions. Let's get started.

OPPOSING VIEWPOINTS® SERIES

Chapter 1

What Is the Current State of Animal Rights?

Chapter Preface

The issue of animal rights and animal welfare has been an important part of the cultural conversation for many years. Activists have used a variety of methods, including both protests and education, to advocate for the rights of animals and to try to improve their living conditions. However, progress has been uneven both within nations and around the world. In some countries, animal rights advocates have made a great deal of progress. In others, not so much. In some places, the movement even seems to be losing ground.

In this opening chapter, the authors take a variety of approaches to the question "What is the current state of animal rights throughout the world?" One author compares nations across the globe to see how each ranks when scored on how well it respects the welfare of animals. (Spoiler: The United States and Canada do not come out on top.) This piece also grapples with the issue of how difficult it is to measure the state of animal welfare.

Another focuses on just the United States, and particularly on how farm animals are protected (or not protected) by U.S. law. A third centers on recent landmark legislation in the United Kingdom that declares some animals have sentience. To the surprise of many, this law extends protection based on sentience not just to mammals, but to other animals such as lobsters and shrimp.

Other authors here dive into the history of the animal rights movement, and even explore how people throughout history have thought about and treated animals.

The first viewpoint gets us started by outlining the history of the animal rights movement and explaining why the concept of animal "rights" is different from the notion of animal "welfare." It's an important distinction, and a good one to keep in mind as you read the essays not only in this chapter but throughout this volume.

Viewpoint 1

> *"Existing laws routinely fail to provide animals with adequate protection. In many cases, the underlying motivation for animal cruelty legislation is exclusively human interest."*

History and Facts about the Animal Rights Movement

karol orzechowski

In this viewpoint, the author discusses the complex concept of animal rights and outlines the goals of the animal rights movement. He also provides some history of the movement and details about some current animal protection laws. The author, who intentionally spells his name without capital letters, is an animal advocate and documentary filmmaker based in Ontario, Canada.

"The Animal Rights Movement: History and Facts About Animal Rights," by karol orzechowski, Faunalytics, April 9, 2020. Reprinted by permission.

As you read, consider the following questions:

1. What is the difference between animal welfare and animal rights?
2. What, according to orzechowski, is the ultimate goal of the animal rights movement?
3. What barriers facing the animal rights movement are discussed in this viewpoint?

Most people would agree that a dog has more sentience than a kitchen table. However, under the eyes of most contemporary legal systems, the two are essentially indistinguishable. While the words "animal rights" can be polarizing, at its core the movement is about gaining legal and public respect for the other species we share this planet with.

Not to be confused with welfare, which entrenches the concept that animals ought to be used for human purposes, the issue at the core of animal rights boils down to the difference between being a *who* and a *what*; a *someone* and a *something*. Are animals resources for human benefit? Or are they sensitive beings who have emotions and preferences and awareness of themselves? The animal rights movement strives to create a more equitable world in which animals are treated with more kindness, understanding and respect.

Do Animals Have Rights?

The question of whether animals have rights is complex. On the one hand, in most countries around the world, there are no laws protecting the rights of animals, or laws that acknowledge the existence of these rights. Therefore it cannot be said that animals have legally recognized or protected rights.

However another way of looking at the existence of animal rights is to suggest that animals have inherent value, which is independent of their value to humans.

In today's world, there is widespread agreement that human beings possess inherent value, even though this value may not always be applied equally, which is the result of racism, patriarchy, and other forms of oppression. Generally speaking, however, inherent value is what renders a being worthy of moral consideration. The inherent value of human beings is calculated according to cognitive and emotional qualities such as our possession of self-awareness, the ability to make conscious decisions and act upon personal preferences, and the fact that we are actively invested in the quality of our own lives. Together, these qualities render us as "subjects of a life"—meaning we possess an active inner world along with an awareness of the external. This awareness renders us particularly vulnerable to harm; since it matters to us when we are harmed. Thanks to the qualities of our consciousness, human beings possess naturally-occurring rights that are legally enshrined in many countries, with the underlying understanding that it is wrong to harm someone who is aware and therefore suffers because of the harm caused.

In Western thought, it was long believed that animals weren't sufficiently aware to notice if they were harmed, that harm simply wouldn't matter to them. Understandings have changed in recent decades. A wealth of established scientific discoveries and anecdotal evidence indicating that certain species are also subjects of a life—meaning they possess the qualities of consciousness human rights protect—show that other species have inherent value and therefore also possess naturally-occurring rights. In this factoring, it is not up to humans to bestow rights onto animals, but simply to recognize and respect these existing rights, through moral and legal frameworks.

When legal animal rights are discussed, it is not suggested that any other-than-human animal be given all the same rights as human beings, such as the right to an education or to vote in elections. Instead, the rights referred to tend to be the basic rights of freedom from confinement, freedom from bodily injury, and freedom to pursue their lives as they wish.

Why Are Animal Rights Important?

Animals are increasingly understood as suffering from psychological, emotional, and physical pain. For example, orcas can suffer from depression and boredom in aquariums, leading to the use of antidepressant drugs. Animals in zoos frequently display stereotypic behaviors, which signify underlying psychological distress and are unseen in wild populations. The more that is learned about the myriad ways our behavior, lifestyles and attitudes negatively impact animals, the greater our moral obligation towards them becomes.

Besides the fact that animals can suffer, the sheer scale of animal exploitation is another reason animal rights are urgently needed. It is estimated that roughly 200 million animals are killed for human consumption every day, with wealthy nations such as Australia, the United States and Europe leading the way with the highest consumption of meat per capita. The U.S. is also responsible for the rise of industrial animal agriculture, in which animals are forced to endure lifetimes of heartbreaking abuse.

What Are the Goals of the Animal Rights Movement?

The ultimate goal of the animal rights movement is to place animals "beyond use" of human beings, putting an end to exploitative industries and practices including laboratory testing, whaling, and puppy mills.

There are many approaches to achieving these goals. Grassroots advocacy, involving public demonstrations, as well as documentaries and other educational tools have long been deployed as methods of raising public awareness of the suffering endured by animals at human hands, as well as familiarizing the public with the concept of animal rights.

Innovative legal approaches have been explored as well. The Nonhuman Rights Project advocates for nonhuman personhood, which is a way to circumvent the legal definition of animals as being property, which denies them legal standing. A nonhuman person, however, may be represented in court via a *guardian ad litem* in order to fight for justice on their behalf.

Another tactic for achieving the goals of the animal rights movement is to advocate for veganism, which is a lifestyle that eliminates consumption of any product derived from animals—including milk, eggs, and insect-derived products like honey. Vegans also avoid clothing derived from animals such as leather, fur and silk. Through widespread adoption of vegan values, the demand for animal products can be reduced, enabling a clearer path to acceptance of animal rights both in popular opinion as well as the reduction in financial incentives to exploit animals.

When Did the Animal Rights Movement Begin?

In some form or another, the concept of animal rights has been around for thousands of years. In Eastern religions such as Buddhism, Hinduism, and Jainism, the concept of *ahimsa*, meaning non-violence, is a central principle. Jainism stresses non-cruelty towards animals, prohibiting adherents from working at a zoo, cutting trees, or using any fabrics, including silk, which are produced through harming other living beings.

Within Europe and North America, there were many precursors of the modern-day animal rights movement. The first animal cruelty legislation was passed in 1635, which prohibited tearing wool off of living sheep. In 1822, Richard Martin, known as "Humanity Dick", passed Martin's Act aimed at preventing cruelty towards cattle. Martin went on to be one of the founding members of the Royal Society for the Prevention of Cruelty to Animals, the world's first animal welfare charity, in 1824.

The first explicit reference to the concept of animal rights came from Henry Stephens Salt, whose book *Animals' Rights: Considered in Relation to Social Progress* rallied against the idea of prejudice against animals. Salt's urging of a recognition for "the common bond of humanity that unites all living beings into one universal brotherhood" echoed ancient religious traditions such as Jainism.

Who Started the Animal Rights Movement?

The animal rights movement was not begun by any one person, though there were certain seminal figures. Although women comprise the majority of animal rights activists and are less likely to support animal exploitation than men, the majority of the credit for starting the animal rights movement is, unfortunately, given to white men. Richard Ryder is among the well-known figures in modern times, having coined the term *speciesism* in 1970 to describe human chauvinism towards other species. In 1975, Peter Singer's *Animal Liberation* was highly influential and lauded, yet he credited some of his views to the comparatively little-known author Ruth Harrison, whose 1964 book *Animal Machines* documented conditions on factory farms.

What Laws Protect Animal Rights?

Because the legal rights of animals are generally not recognized, federal and state laws in the United States pertain to welfare instead of rights. These laws regard animals as property and deal with "unnecessary" harm to animals, thereby allowing for a great deal of suffering which is deemed "necessary" or justifiable.

Existing laws routinely fail to provide animals with adequate protection. In many cases, the underlying motivation for animal cruelty legislation is exclusively human interest. U.S. federal laws regarding animal protection include the Animal Welfare Act (AWA), enacted in 1966 out of concern for cats and dogs used in laboratory research, though its contemporary mandate includes a wider realm of animal exploitation issues including animals in entertainment and captive breeding. However the AWA excludes hunting, fishing and trapping, slaughter of animals, retail pet stores, and others from its jurisdiction. The AWA is far from being an anti-cruelty law; for example, it regulates—meaning, does not render illegal—the practise of vivisection, which is surgery conducted on a living animal during research. In laboratories, the AWA does not protect animals from harm during the course of research, nor does it prohibit their use.

Incredibly, the definition of "animals" in the AWA excludes mice, birds, rats and agricultural animals—who are the most heavily exploited animals across the country, within laboratories and industrial agriculture operations.

Other federal laws pertaining to animals include the Endangered Species Act, which maintains a list of species around the world who are threatened or endangered and outlines procedures as well as penalties for their inappropriate use. The Preventing Animal Cruelty and Torture Act bans intentional cruelty onto animals, though it excludes animals in agriculture including slaughter, as well as hunting, fishing, trapping, medical research, pest control and other abuses.

Facts About Animal Rights

- In the U.S., every circus that uses animals has been cited by the Animal Welfare Act for violations.
- The California Orca Protection Act prohibits keeping orcas captive throughout the state. In Canada, a nationwide ban on cetacean captivity was also passed.
- Joaquin Phoenix used his speech at the Oscars to talk about animal rights.

Animal Rights Barriers to Success

Financial incentives form a significant barrier to animal rights, since it is through their consideration as property that animals' exploitation is enabled. Animal business is big business. In the United States alone, the pet industry topped $221.1 billion in 2015; the live animal trade accounted for $3.5 billion in 2016; in 2020, animal agriculture is forecasted to bring in $185.8 billion in cash receipts. Companies may go to great lengths to protect profits, and have lobbied successfully for legislation such as ag-gag laws which conceal the unsavory conditions within their facilities in order to continue operating unencumbered by negative public perception or stricter anti-cruelty regulation.

Dependence on animal products is another barrier to the success of the movement. Animal products can be found throughout modern Western societies and in places people may least expect. For example, parts of pigs are found in everyday objects such as concrete, paint, soap, collagen injections, and even bullets.

Cultural beliefs about animals form yet another barrier to the success of the movement. For example, patriarchal conceptions of manhood assert that in order to be a strong, virile man, one must eat large quantities of meat, especially red meat such as steak. Sport hunting and fishing, and other similar "conquest"-type activities, lie at the heart of hegemonic manhood identities that are at odds with animal rights.

Threats

Globalization Affecting the Movement

Within neoliberal capitalism, animals are considered commodities. So-called advancements in technology, such as CAFOs [concentrated animal feeding operations], along with increased connectivity and market reach perpetuated by globalization can be linked with drastically increased numbers of animals exploited, coupled with tumbling standards of welfare. Government officials in the UK have openly expressed resistance to "US-style farming", which would see an influx of CAFO operations in the country. CAFOs have already spread to many other countries, such as India, China and Japan. Ultimately, globalization tends to entrench the use of animals, leaving little to no room for discourse regarding rights or even increased welfare protections.

While globalization brings increased connection between individuals and organizations within the animal rights movement itself, there are some concerns related to how these networks are fostered. Organizations based in North America and Europe that conduct international outreach efforts and resource deployment can, at times, engage in behavioral patterns that entrench ongoing legacies of colonialism. Ways beyond these problems include hiring locally, placing people of color in leadership roles and taking the local context into account within campaigning strategies.

Science

Scientific approaches can reflect the logic and biases of human exceptionalism within the selection of questions to be investigated, experimental design and interpretations of findings.

One example of such a bias is that it is impossible to know with absolute certainty what an other-than-human animal is thinking or feeling, and that they therefore cannot be proven as thinking or feeling at all. This assumption is frequently used to justify the ongoing exploitation of animals. The burden of proof is foisted onto those humans who oppose this assumption and onto the animals themselves, requiring that they communicate, unequivocally and in human language, that they are in fact subjects of a life—that is, that they experience emotions, possess desires, and so on. However, some argue that the burden of proof should rest upon those skeptical of animals being subjects of a life. And in light of the abundant concrete and anecdotal evidence of animals' inner lives, proving otherwise would actually be impossible.

Co-option

Animal exploitation industries have largely co-opted the concepts of animal welfare and humane treatment, in order to continue exploiting animals. While these ideals may have originally been intended to protect animals from harm, industries have successfully managed to apply these words to product labels and processes in order to assuage consumers while hiding the underbelly of industrial agriculture. Now, wherever these words are present, they more indicate animal abuse than anything else.

What Is Needed for the Success of Animal Rights?

For animal rights to become legally recognized in Western culture, there needs to be a broad cultural shift across many sectors. People will need to understand and accept that animals are thinking, feeling beings who are not put on this earth for humanity's use. Speciesism must fade away, along with outdated scientific and philosophical ideas that animals are nothing more than mindless automatons. Patriarchal conceptions of manhood must be dismantled. Forward-thinking legislators must set precedents that pave the way for legal rights.

Fortunately, there is movement towards a more equitable world for animals; for example, plant-based diets are becoming increasingly popular; bans on fur are being enacted; and laboratories are turning towards alternatives to animals.

Conclusion

There is still a long road ahead before the animal rights movement achieves the ultimate goal of legally enshrining rights for other-than-human animals. Fortunately, progress is being made in Western countries and around the world, though it may be incremental. As people come to understand more about animals and the suffering they endure at human hands, hopefully the change will only accelerate.

Viewpoint 2

> *"Most countries are not doing very much to protect and promote the welfare of animals."*

The World Still Has a Long Way to Go to Protect Animal Welfare

Seth Millstein

Keeping up with how well various countries are protecting animals is difficult. Here, the author discusses methods of ranking countries and shares the results of two types of rankings. Seth Millstein is a writer and musician living in the Bay Area. He has helped launch several early-stage journalism startups.

"The Best & Worst Countries for Animal Welfare Are Difficult to Measure" by Seth Millstein, August 6th, 2024. This story was originally published by Sentient Media: https://sentientmedia.org/best-and-worst-countries-for-animal-rights/. Reprinted by permission.

As you read, consider the following questions:

1. Why is it so difficult to measure animal welfare?
2. What methods of measuring animal welfare does Millstein discuss here?
3. Why are the API rankings of Ethiopia, Kenya, Tanzania, Niger and Nigeria misleading, according to this viewpoint?

The general concept of animal welfare may seem fairly straightforward. But efforts to measure animal welfare, however, are far more complicated. Attempting to identify the best and worst countries for animal welfare is no easy task, but a close look at the work of several organizations advocating for animal rights gives us an idea of which places treat animals the best—and the worst.

Measuring Animal Welfare: No Easy Task

Many things can contribute to or detract from the welfare of any given country's animals, and there's no single or unified way of measuring all of them.

You could, for instance, compare the total number of animals slaughtered in each country every year. There's an intuitive appeal to this approach, as slaughtering an animal is the ultimate way of diminishing his or her welfare.

But raw death tolls, informative as they are, omit several other important factors. The living conditions of farm animals before they're slaughtered is a big determinant of their welfare, for example, as is the method of slaughter and the manner in which they're transported to slaughterhouses.

Moreover, not all animal suffering takes place within industrialized agriculture in the first place. Pollution and environmental degradation, cosmetics testing, illegal animal fights, cruelty to pets and many other practices also hurt animal welfare, and aren't captured in raw animal death statistics.

Another potential way of measuring the state of animal welfare in a country is by looking at what laws it has on the books protecting animals—or, alternatively, perpetuating their harm. This is the method used by the Animal Protection Index (API), one of the sources we'll be referring to later on.

What Determines Animal Welfare in a Country?

Laws that punish animal cruelty by individuals, regulate the treatment of animals in factory farms and slaughterhouses, forbid environmental destruction that harm animals and recognize animal sentience can all increase the animal welfare in a country. On the other hand, laws that effectively enable the mistreatment of animals, such as ag-gag laws in some U.S. states, will result in worse animal welfare.

But in any given country, there are many, many, many different laws that can potentially affect animal welfare, and there's no objective way of determining which of these laws "matter" more than others. Just as important is law enforcement: animal protections aren't much good if they aren't enforced, so looking solely at laws on the books can also be misleading.

In theory, one excellent way to assess animal welfare in a country would be to look at the religious and cultural attitudes towards animals in that country. But attitudes can't be quantitatively measured, and even if they could, they don't always align with actual behavior.

The aforementioned metrics all have upsides and downsides. To overcome this challenge, the animal welfare group Voiceless developed the Voiceless Animal Cruelty Index (VACI), a hybrid approach for measuring animal welfare. The system uses three different categories for grading a country's level of animal welfare: Producing Cruelty, Consuming Cruelty and Sanctioning Cruelty.

Producing Cruelty measures the number of animals that a country slaughters for food every year, but on a per-capita basis to account for different countries' population sizes. The totals here also factor into the ranking of each country, in an attempt to account for the treatment of the animals before they're slaughtered.

The second category, Consuming Cruelty, looks at a country's rate of meat and dairy consumption, again on a per-capita basis. It uses two metrics to measure this: the ratio of farmed animal protein consumption to plant-based protein consumption in the country, and an estimation of the total number of animals consumed per person.

Finally, Sanctioning Cruelty looks at the laws and regulations each country has surrounding animal welfare, and is based on the welfare rankings on the API.

Before getting into the rankings, it should be noted both Voiceless and the Animal Protection Index only looked at 50 countries. The countries selected are collectively home to 80 percent of farmed animals worldwide, and while there are practical reasons for this methodological limitation, it does mean that the results come with some caveats, which we'll go into later.

Which Countries Are the Best for Animal Welfare?

The VACI's Rankings

Using the aforementioned criteria, the VACI says that the following countries have the highest levels of animal welfare. They are, in order:

- Tanzania (tied)
- India (tied)
- Kenya
- Nigeria
- Sweden (tied)
- Switzerland (tied)
- Austria
- Ethiopia (tied)
- Niger (tied)
- The Philippines

The API's Rankings

The API uses a slightly broader assessment, assigning each country a letter grade for its treatment of animals. The letters go from A to G; unfortunately, none of the countries received an "A," but several received a "B" or a "C."

The following countries were given a "B:"

- Austria
- Denmark
- The Netherlands
- Sweden
- Switzerland
- The United Kingdom

The below countries were given a "C" for their treatment of animals:

- New Zealand
- India
- Mexico
- Malaysia
- France
- Germany
- Italy
- Poland
- Spain

Which Countries Are the Worst for Animal Welfare?

The VACI and API also listed the countries that they deem the worst for animal welfare.

Here they are, in descending order of badness, on the VACI:

- Australia (tied)
- Belarus (tied)
- The United States
- Argentina (tied)
- Myanmar (tied)

- Iran
- Russia
- Brazil
- Morocco
- Chile

The API, meanwhile, gave two countries a "G" rating for animal welfare—the lowest possible grade—and seven more countries an "F," the second worst grade. Here are those rankings:

- Iran (G)
- Azerbaijan (G)
- Belarus (F)
- Algeria (F)
- Egypt (F)
- Ethiopia (F)
- Morocco (F)
- Myanmar (F)
- Vietnam (F)

Why the Discrepancies in Rankings for Animal Welfare?

As we can see, there's a decent amount of agreement between the two rankings. Switzerland, Sweden and Austria all rank highly on both lists, and although India received a significantly lower grade on the API, its welfare ranking still places it in the top 30 percent of countries assessed.

There's even more overlap regarding the worst countries for animal welfare, with Iran, Belarus, Morocco and Myanmar all ranking very low on both lists.

But there are some significant discrepancies as well. Perhaps most notable is Ethiopia: according to the VACI, it's one of the best countries in the world for animals, but the API says it's one of the worst.

Tanzania, Kenya and several other African countries that received high marks on the VACI were given moderate-to-poor grades on the API. Denmark and the Netherlands ranked high on the Animal Protection Index, but were below average in the VACI rankings.

So, why all the discrepancies? There are several answers to this question, and all are illuminating in their own ways.

Ethiopia, Kenya, Tanzania, Niger and Nigeria all ranked relatively low on the API, indicating that they have weak animal welfare laws and regulations. While that's nothing to celebrate, it's also outweighed by two other factors: farming methods and meat consumption rates.

In all of the above countries, factory farms are rare or non-existent, and animal farming is instead small-scale and extensive. Much of the suffering livestock around the world experience is due to the common practices of factory farms; small-scale extensive farming, by contrast, provides animals with more living space and basic amenities, and thus significantly reduces their misery.

In addition, the aforementioned African countries all have very low levels of meat, dairy and milk consumption. Ethiopia is an especially striking example: its residents consume fewer animals per person than any other country on the list, and its per-capita animal consumption is just 10 percent of the global average.

As a result, significantly fewer farm animals are killed annually in the above countries, and this increases the overall level of animal welfare.

In the Netherlands, meanwhile, something like the reverse is true. The country has some of the strongest animal welfare laws on the planet, but it produces and consumes a sizable amount of animal products, which partially diminishes the impact of its strong anti-cruelty laws.

The Bottom Line

The agreements and discrepancies between the VACI and API rankings highlight an important fact: whether we're talking about countries, cities or people, there are a lot of qualities that can't be measured on a single spectrum. Animal welfare is one of

Animal Rights Activists May Not Be Who You Think They Are

Animal rights activist. The stereotype is of a flaky do-gooder out to grant animals the rights to drive a car, vote in an election and have a fair and speedy trial. But animal rights activists do not see animals as humans. Rather, they emphasize that humans are animals and should not impose their will onto other animals for humans' supposed benefit. Animal rights theorists argue that animal exploitation industries are detrimental to human health and the environment. They believe animals should not be caged or used for entertainment (as in zoos, circuses and rodeos) and seek to abolish all animal use and exploitation (as in the pet trade and the fur and silk industry). If human animals cannot ethically and legally kill each other, then they should not feel ethically and legally justified killing other animals. They argue that non-human animals are creatures with complex social networks and desires to pursue happiness and objectives and should be treated as such.

. . .

The modern animal rights movement began in the 1970s when ethicist Peter Singer published *Animal Liberation*. The book quickly gathered international attention and inspired many people to lead cruelty-free lifestyles. The animal rights movement escalated in the U.S. during the 1980s as several high profile campaigns caught the attention of the media. A number of cosmetic giants stopped testing on animals after one campaign. Another brought record losses and an irreparably tarnished public image to the fur industry. In the 1990s grassroots activism took a leading role in determining the direction of the movement. At college campuses across the country, students engaged in acts of civil disobedience to protest campus vivisection and local fur shops. As the movement enters the 21st century vegetarian/vegan options are on most menus, animal rights is taught in schools and the ideology has become a permanent fixture on our cultural landscape. People from all walks of life now have the opportunity to get involved and be a part of a movement that is making advances for those animals suffering from human exploitation.

"Animal Rights: Past and Present" by Kevin Kjonnas, Do It Green! Minnesota.

them; while we can come up with a rough ranking of countries, no list of "the 10 best countries for animal welfare" is definitive, comprehensive or free of caveats.

The API's list also reveals another truth: most countries are not doing very much to protect and promote the welfare of animals. It's notable that not a single country received an "A" grade from API, implying that even the countries with the most progressive laws on animal welfare, such as the Netherlands, still have a way to go to truly promote the wellbeing of their animals.

Viewpoint 3

> *"The animal rights movement has accomplished several significant changes and advancements over the years ..."*

The Notion of Animal Rights Is Not New

Selina Darlim

The author opens this viewpoint by discussing ancient attitudes towards animals, some of which were very concerned with animal welfare. She then goes on to talk about the history of the animal rights movement. Selina Darlim is a wildlife conservationist and animal rights advocate who often writes for nonprofits and media.

"Animal Rights Movement: Understanding When and Why It Started" by Selena Darlim, Animal Charity Evaluators, https://animalcharityevaluators.org/blog/animal-rights-movement/, August 28, 2023. Reprinted by permission.

As you read, consider the following questions:

1. What effect did Upton Sinclair's novel *The Jungle* have on public attitudes in the US about animals?
2. How has the animal rights movement change over time?
3. What challenges does the animal rights movement still face, according to this article?

The animal rights movement has progressed with time, reflecting our growing knowledge of animals' needs and changing attitudes toward their treatment. What can animal advocates learn from looking back at how the animal rights movement came to be? In this article, we'll explore the concept of animal rights and the history of the animal rights movement, delving into its early days, goals, challenges, and evolution in the modern era.

Do Animals Have Rights?

The belief that nonhuman animals have intrinsic value and the right to be treated with respect and compassion has existed in some form for millennia. For example, the Indian principle of *ahiṃsā*, which preaches nonviolence toward all living beings, dates back to the 9th century BCE and is observed in religions such as Hinduism, Buddhism, and Jainism to this day. Throughout history, however, humans have generally regarded animals as commodities with no inherent rights. One of the first prominent figures to discuss animals' moral value, 17th-century French philosopher René Descartes, promoted a particularly callous view of animals. He argued that animals lacked a mind and could not feel pain, justifying cruel acts such as live vivisection. This sentiment fortunately lost favor as humans' understanding of animal cognition, emotions, and sentience deepened.

Why Are Animal Rights Important?

Animals are sentient beings capable of experiencing pain, suffering, and joy. Respecting their rights to not be harmed, captured, taken away from their habitat, abused, confined, or killed for human purposes is in line with moral principles such as empathy, compassion, and ethical conduct. By securing animal rights, we can greatly minimize the amount of pain and suffering in the world. Acknowledging animal rights also benefits humans. For example, improving the living conditions of animals on farms decreases the likelihood of disease transmission to humans. Similarly, reducing meat consumption can help curb the impact of climate change and preserve ecosystems.

When Did the Animal Rights Movement Start?

The modern-day animal rights movement traces back to the Industrial Revolution, when rapid industrialization and urbanization spurred massive changes across Europe and North America. Along with other industries, traditional farming practices were replaced by large-scale, profit-driven factory farms and slaughterhouses. The dangerous, unsanitary, and traumatic working conditions in these meat industry facilities were famously depicted in Upton Sinclair's 1906 book *The Jungle*. People began to question the treatment of workers and animals in this new industrial era, leading to the first organized animal advocacy efforts.

Who Started the First Animal Rights Movement?

Several people played a role in the development of the animal rights movement, although a few individuals are often credited with starting it. One of these individuals is Richard Martin, an Irish politician who passed one of the first farmed animal welfare laws (the Cruel Treatment of Cattle Act) in 1822 and founded the first animal welfare charity (the Royal Society for the Prevention of Cruelty to Animals) in 1824. Another prominent figure of the early animal rights movement is Henry Stephens Salt, an English writer and social reformer who argued in favor of animal rights in his 1892 book *Animals' Rights: Considered in Relation to Social Progress.*

What Are the Goals of the Animal Rights Movement?

The goals of the animal rights movement have evolved over time, with early efforts more focused on soliciting compassion for animals and modern efforts more focused on reducing animal consumption or securing legal protection. Today, the end goal of the animal rights movement is to abolish all human activities that cause animal suffering, including factory farming, animal experimentation, and habitat destruction. Animal rights advocates focus on various causes and use different approaches to achieve this goal.

What Laws Protect Animal Rights?

Animal rights laws vary significantly among countries, states, and jurisdictions. Although most countries still do not recognize animal rights or sentience, several have implemented laws to protect certain species against cruelty and neglect. Laws range from basic anti-cruelty protections to more nuanced regulations designed to address animal treatment in specific contexts. Companion animals tend to receive greater protection than farmed and wild animals, as industries routinely challenge new and existing legislation.

Was the Animal Rights Movement Successful?

Although there have been considerable advancements in animal welfare, the animal rights movement still faces challenges. Legal and societal shifts have resulted in better protections against animal cruelty and exploitation, but enforcement remains weak, welfare considerations for farmed animals are lacking, and few countries officially recognize animal sentience in law. Nevertheless, the movement has made significant progress by banning certain cruel practices, improving living conditions for animals, and shifting public opinion.

What Did the Animal Rights Movement Accomplish?

The animal rights movement has accomplished several significant changes and advancements over the years, although the extent of these accomplishments varies by species and region. Some notable accomplishments of the animal rights movement include:

- Raising public awareness about the treatment of animals in various industries, such as factory farming, entertainment, and research
- Influencing the creation and enforcement of laws and regulations aimed at protecting animals, covering areas such as animal cruelty, animal testing, and wildlife conservation
- Improving conditions for farmed animals in some regions, with some companies and farms adopting more humane practices, larger enclosures, and better living conditions for animals
- Addressing issues like poaching, illegal wildlife trade, and the use of animals in entertainment
- Pressuring companies to adopt more ethical and sustainable sources in their supply chains

The growth of the animal rights movement has also resulted in increased collaboration with other causes, such as environmental protection, social justice, labor rights, and human health. This approach addresses the broader context in which animal suffering occurs and builds alliances for more effective advocacy.

When Did Effective Animal Advocacy Emerge?

Effective animal advocacy (EAA) emerged during the early days of Effective Altruism (EA), a movement that uses evidence and reason to identify the most efficient and impactful ways to do good. EA gained prominence in the 21st century and quickly spread to philanthropic spaces, including the animal rights movement. The first group solely dedicated to effective animal advocacy, Effective Animal Activism, was founded in 2012 as an intern project of 80,000 Hours—a U.K.-based organization that guides individuals toward high-impact careers. Effective Animal Activism sought to improve animal welfare as much as possible, despite the lack of evidence-based guidance on the most effective ways to do so.

Growth of Effective Animal Advocacy

Effective Animal Activism's earliest efforts consisted of evaluating animal charities, expanding the effective animal advocacy community, and providing career advice to aspiring animal advocates. In 2013, the group merged with a 501(c)(3) nonprofit and revised its mission to finding and promoting highly effective opportunities to help animals, soon rebranding as Animal Charity Evaluators (ACE). Charity evaluations became ACE's core, and we remained the most prominent organization in EAA for years. Through introspection and the growth of EAA, we realized the limitations of our approach in directing funds to smaller groups in underrepresented regions. To address this gap, we introduced the Movement Grants Program.

How Did Effective Animal Advocacy Impact the Animal Rights Movement?

Effective animal advocacy has influenced the animal rights movement by popularizing data-driven approaches with measurable impact, leading to more strategic and cost-effective advocacy efforts. Despite its positive impacts, EAA has also been criticized for its quantitative focus, lack of diversity, prioritization methods, and association with the EA movement. As a prominent figure in the EAA space, ACE carefully considers these critiques and continually reassesses our approach to ensure we support the entire animal rights movement as best we can.

Conclusion

From ancient principles of nonviolence to modern legal debates, the animal rights movement is larger and more relevant than ever before. While many challenges lie ahead, the movement's forward progress is undeniable. Will you help us advance it even further?

> *"Understanding animal sentience and which species possess it is essential in promoting better animal welfare, but providing healthy and sustainable habitats is also vital for wild animals."*

The UK Is a Leader in Animal Welfare

Andrew Rowan

This article provides detail and context for the UK's Animal Sentience Act. It was passed to address the gap in animal welfare law that was left when the UK left the European Union. Andrew Rowan is a longstanding expert in animal welfare science and animal and environmental advocacy. He is president of the board of directors of WellBeing International.

"UK Passes Its Own Animal Sentience Act After Leaving EU," by Andrew Rowan, WellBeing International, May 2, 2022. Reprinted by permission.

As you read, consider the following questions:

1. How is the UK law different from that of the EU?
2. Why do you think the law particularly forbids rodent glue traps?
3. What, according to the viewpoint, is the connection between animal welfare and environmental protection?

When the UK (United Kingdom) voted to leave the European Union (EU), one of the consequences would be the loss of legislation on various issues covered in existing EU laws. The UK government had to pass new laws covering the many items in EU legislation that would no longer apply to the UK, including the statement in the EU governing treaty that animals were sentient. The Conservative Government had promised to address the complicated range of legislative gaps, including the declaration that animals are sentient beings, that would be precipitated by the UK's departure from the EU via new omnibus legislation. As expected, the very complicated omnibus EU-departure legislation did not address all the "gap" issues. In particular, the issue of animal sentience was omitted. This omission prompted public dismay that animals would no longer have the protection of the EU declaration that they were sentient beings and led to a campaign calling on the Government to correct the omission. The Government promised to do so and eventually developed an Animal Welfare (Sentience) Bill to take the place of the EU language. On April 28, 2022, the United Kingdom (UK) Government bill stating that animals are sentient received Royal Assent from Queen Elizabeth, meaning that the bill is now an Act, the law of the land. What does this new law mean in practice?

The United Kingdom's animal sentience legislative approach is different from that adopted by the EU. On the issue of animal sentience, the EU included a declaration that animals were sentient in the treaty that governs the functioning of the EU (Article 13) but did not develop a process for enforcing the declaration. By contrast, the new UK act has no declaration but does outline a process whereby government departments will be held accountable for including animal sentience in their deliberations and policies. In the words of Professor Jonathan Birch of the London School of Economics (and an advisor to the UK Government on the animal sentience issue):

> *The UK has an approach to animal welfare based on oversight and accountability, with processes already in place to make sure scientists and farmers take welfare into account. This new Act extends that approach to policymakers themselves. Now they too have a duty to regard animals as sentient beings, and a process will be put in place to hold them to account before Parliament if they neglect that duty.*

The new law does not include a definition of "sentience" but leaves it up to the Government to decide which animals qualify as sentient. The Royal Society for the Prevention of Cruelty to Animals has developed a working definition of sentience as the "capacity to experience positive and negative feelings such as pleasure, joy, pain, and distress that matter to the individual." The Government has now decided that the new bill will apply to a broader range of creatures than the vertebrates who have traditionally been considered to be sentient.

The new UK Animal Sentience Act applies to all vertebrates and decapod crustaceans (e.g., lobsters, crabs, and shrimp) and cephalopod mollusks such as the octopus. Cephalopod suffering and distress have already been recognized in some circumstances (e.g., animal experimentation laws and regulations). The new UK Animal Sentience Act will raise challenging issues regarding treating "farmed" octopuses and standard practices such as killing lobsters by placing them alive and conscious in boiling water.

Farming octopus has become an issue only recently. The Spanish multinational corporation, Nueva Pescanova, announced that it plans to start marketing farmed octopus (raised on an octopus "farm" in the Canary Islands) in 2023. While octopus farming may help reduce the pressure on wild octopus populations (an estimated 350,000 tonnes caught annually—ten times the amount caught in 1950), the increasing global concern regarding octopus sentience may put a hitch in the company's plans.

The UK prides itself on being a leader in animal welfare, and the new Sentience Act confirms that leadership. The UK also has a government minister (Lord Zac Goldsmith) responsible for an animal welfare portfolio. The press release that announced the Queen's approval of the Animal Sentience bill also announced a bill outlawing rodent glue traps—a particularly problematic device from the perspective of animal welfare. The press release noted that the UK, since leaving the EU, "has been able to strengthen further its position as a global leader on animal rights." The Government has also published an Action Plan for Animal Welfare. It promises to focus on five key areas—sentience and enforcement, international trade and advocacy, farm animals, pets and sporting animals, and wild animals. It will be interesting to follow how the Sentience Act now plays out in practical policies and laws in the UK.

In particular, the Sentience Act could have some far-reaching implications for wild animals and the protection of wild vertebrate (and invertebrate) habitats. Wild animals require healthy habitats and healthy environments to thrive. The Royal Society for the Protection of Birds (RSPB) in the UK produces an annual State of the Birds report, documenting a 55% decline in populations of farmland bird species and a 27% decline in populations of woodland bird species. The decline in farmland birds has occurred despite the widespread uptake of agri-environment schemes in the UK. Overall, there were just over 80 million breeding pairs of birds in the UK or 19 million fewer pairs of native breeding birds in 2017 compared to 1966.

Understanding animal sentience and which species possess it is essential in promoting better animal welfare, but providing healthy and sustainable habitats is also vital for wild animals. A new NGO, the Wild Animal Initiative (founded in 2017), highlights the issues adversely affecting wildlife and campaigns to improve the welfare of wild animals (more than just wild animal conservation).

There have been relatively few practical consequences of the various declarations in laws and public policy that animals are sentient. The new UK Animal Welfare (Sentience) Act will probably change that. The Act establishes an expert committee responsible for ensuring that government policy includes appropriate attention to animal sentience. Government ministers will be required to provide formal responses to questions raised by the new committee. This oversight process will likely raise many difficult questions about animal treatment in the years to come. It will undoubtedly begin to answer specific practical questions about the definition of sentience and the range of sentient animals.

Viewpoint 5

> *"Federal and state laws not only fall short of protecting farmed animals, they actively serve the interests of industrial animal agriculture."*

US Laws Do Little to Protect Animals Most in Need of Protection

Staff of the New Roots Institute

In this piece, the authors focus mostly on farm animals. While there are some protections, these animals enjoy very few protections, and those are often subject to exceptions. The New Roots Institute is a nonprofit that aims to end factory farming.

"What Are the Laws That Protect Animals and Their Rights?," New Roots Staff, New Roots Institute, May 31, 2022. Reprinted by permission.

As you read, consider the following questions:

1. What do the authors mean by the "distinction between friends and food" and why does that mean farm animals are typically left with no legal protections?
2. The authors here list several exceptions to laws that protect farm animals. What are the reasons behind these exceptions? Do those seem reasonable?
3. What interests are the laws discussed here intended to protect, according to this viewpoint?

There are few laws that protect animals from cruelty, and even fewer for farmed animals like cows, chickens, and pigs.

Puppies and piglets have a lot in common—both are intelligent, loving, playful, and full of personality—yet there is often a huge contrast between the ways that these animals are viewed and treated by humans. Many of us were brought up thinking that dogs are for playing with but pigs are for eating. Despite making no logical or ethical sense, this distinction between friends and food is reflected in anti-cruelty laws, which generally leave farmed animals with next to no legal protection.

How Many Laws Protect Animal Rights?

There are no laws in the U.S. that recognize animals as legal persons who have rights. Laws that protect animals instead focus on animal welfare, which is rooted in the idea that animals should be killed for food, experimented on in labs, and used for other human purposes.

Federal Animal Protection Laws

Several federal laws exist to safeguard the welfare of animals and conserve what are considered to be ecologically important wildlife at the species level, but none of them offer any protection to animals raised for meat, dairy, and eggs.

As we will see below, cows, pigs, and sheep are covered by the 28 Hour Law during transportation and then by the Humane

Slaughter Act once inside the slaughterhouse. Chickens, who make up the overwhelming majority of individual land animals farmed for food, have no federal protection at all.

Horse Protection Act

The Horse Protection Act makes it illegal to transport, show, or sell a horse who has been sored. Soring is the practice of deliberately making a horse's legs or hooves painful so that they will jump higher and run faster in shows. This often involves applying chemical irritants to a horse's legs or cutting too far into a horse's hoof.

The "28 Hour Law"

In theory, under the 28 Hour Law, farmed animals cannot be transported for more than 28 hours at a time without being granted a minimum of five hours off the vehicle to eat, drink, and rest. However, there are several cases in which this does not apply.

The 28 Hour Law only covers animals who are transported by land and who do not have the chance to eat, drink, and rest on the journey. It also does not cover poultry. Beyond that, the time limit can be extended to 36 hours if a written request has been made or, in the case of sheep, if the journey ends at night. In addition, animals can be kept in transit for more than 28 hours without a break if it isn't possible to unload them because of unavoidable circumstances.

According to a report by the Animal Welfare Institute, the 28-hour limit is "rarely enforced." Even when the law is complied with, 28 hours is a long time to stand nose to tail in an overcrowded truck with no access to food or water, especially in freezing or sweltering temperatures.

The Animal Crush Video Prohibition Act

The Animal Crush Video Prohibition Act bans the production, distribution, marketing, sale, and exchange of animal crush videos. Under this legislation, an animal crush video is an obscene image, video, or recording of any form that shows a person deliberately crushing, suffocating, burning, or otherwise physically harming a nonhuman animal. (The act does not apply to videos and images of animal slaughter or other standard farming practices.)

The Animal Welfare Act

The Animal Welfare Act requires that some nonhuman animals used for commercial purposes (e.g. pet stores, zoos) be given a basic level of care. However, it excludes farmed animals raised and killed for food in the U.S.—roughly 10 billion individuals per year. Fish, reptiles and amphibians, invertebrates, animals used in laboratory settings, horses who aren't used in laboratories, and most wild animals are also left unprotected by the act.

The Endangered Species Act

The Endangered Species Act protects animals who are listed as endangered or threatened from being taken from the wild, owned, sold, or transported, with some exceptions. In some instances it also protects the areas where these animals live from being damaged by human activity.

The Humane Slaughter Act

The Humane Methods of Slaughter Act requires that pigs, cattle, sheep, and certain other animals at slaughter facilities be quickly and effectively stunned (gassed, electrocuted, or shot) prior to being killed, except in the case of ritual or religious slaughter. Aside from the obvious problem that there is no "humane" way to take a healthy animal's life, the act also does not offer any protection to chickens and fish and therefore excludes the bulk of individual animals who are slaughtered.

The Lacey Act

The Lacey Act makes it illegal to trade species that have been unlawfully obtained from the wild and was first introduced in 1900, largely to prevent the sale of poached game across state lines, though it now addresses many forms of wildlife-related crime. The law, which applies to plants as well as to animals, also exists to prevent the introduction of non-native wildlife species that have the potential to cause damage to U.S. land and native animals.

The PACT (Preventing Animal Cruelty and Torture) Act

The PACT Act adds to the legislation on animal crush videos, making the violence itself illegal in addition to the production and distribution of the videos.

The Shark Conservation Act

Under the Shark Conservation Act, sharks in the U.S., with the exception of dogfish sharks, can only be brought to shore if their fins remain "naturally attached" to their bodies. This helps to prevent the banned practice of shark finning, which usually involves cutting off a shark's fins at sea and throwing the mutilated shark back into the water to suffer a slow, painful death.

Animal Laws by State

Every state has laws that ban animal cruelty, but what is considered to be an act of cruelty differs across the country, as does the legal definition of an animal. In many cases, state animal protection laws make it illegal to deliberately injure, torture, or take the life of some animals unless as part of normal farming operations. This essentially means that factory farms can legally use inhumane practices that cause immense pain and distress to animals as long as the practices are routine and widespread within the industry.

Oklahoma

In Oklahoma statutes, all nonhuman animals are included in the definition of an "animal." But although farmed animals are at least given minimal legal protections, the law is still heavily biased toward the agricultural corporations that harm them. Local governments in Oklahoma are banned from granting farmed animals any more legal protection than is provided by state law.

New Jersey

In New Jersey statutes, "animal" also seems to refer to all nonhuman animals. However, standard farming practices, along with several other activities, are exempt from anti-cruelty regulations. A farmer who harms an animal in a way that is not considered acceptable also cannot be prosecuted for their first minor offense without first having been given a written warning.

What Animals Are Protected by Law?

Many animals are protected by law, but what these legal protections look like varies widely between groups of animals. Below, we take a look at how the law protects companion animals, farmed animals, and wildlife.

Companion Animals

Widely regarded as friends and family members rather than food, companion cats and dogs are generally far better protected by law than animals we use for other purposes. It is illegal in many parts of the U.S. to leave a dog trapped inside a car in hot weather. And to help address the problem of puppy mills, California, Maryland, and numerous cities and counties across the country have banned the sale of commercially bred companion cats, dogs, and rabbits in pet stores.

Farmed Animals

Recent years have seen significant progress in farmed animal protection laws, such as a number of states banning or limiting the use of some of the most intensive forms of confinement such as gestation crates and battery cages. However, there is still a very long way to go before so-called "food" animals finally get the legal protections they deserve. Even when not kept in cages, factory-farmed animals are denied basic freedoms and routinely subject to acts that would be unlawful to perform on a companion cat or dog, such as castration without anesthesia.

Federal and state laws do not only fall short of protecting farmed animals, they actively serve the interests of industrial animal agriculture. Recent years have seen some states go so far as to pass anti-whistleblower or "ag-gag" laws, which criminalize the work of undercover investigators in order to prevent the harsh realities of factory farming from being made known to the public.

Only the most indefensible acts of cruelty toward farmed animals, for instance attacking them with a pitchfork or kicking an individual who is too sick or injured to move, are widely considered illegal. Even in these cases, justice often isn't served. Given that violence toward animals generally happens behind closed doors, proving that a crime has been committed is anything but easy, and prosecutors aren't always interested in taking on the case. And when an act of cruelty does result in prosecution, the blame often lands on individual workers, who are often unfairly treated themselves, rather than those in charge of the factory farm.

Wildlife

Legal protection for wildlife is mixed. While many ecologically important species and their habitats are protected from harm for conservation purposes, other wild animals are routinely killed for food or for sport. Fishing and hunting are commonly exempt from anti-cruelty laws, as is the killing of so-called "pest" species, which include foxes, coyotes, wolves, rabbits, and many other species.

How Can We Protect Animals?

One of the most effective ways we can protect animals is with our food choices. By swapping meat, dairy, fish, and eggs for plant-based foods, we can gradually reduce the number of animals who are bred to be killed for food. Other actions you can take include talking to your friends, family, and co-workers, writing to your local representatives, supporting animal rights campaigns, supporting organizations working to end factory farming, and volunteering at an animal sanctuary.

Animal Cruelty

Farmed animals need more regulations to protect them from acts of cruelty. Certain farming practices that cause suffering should not be exempt from anti-cruelty laws simply because they are routine. Farmed animals experience pain and can suffer the same as the cats and dogs we welcome into our families and they deserve the same level of protection.

Conclusion

Farmed fish, chickens, pigs, and cows are among the animals most in need of legal protection, yet the few laws that do exist to protect these individuals are woefully lacking and poorly enforced. Anti-cruelty legislation currently does nothing to address factory farming, one of the leading causes of animal suffering on the planet.

Periodical and Internet Sources Bibliography

The following articles have been selected to supplement the diverse views presented in this chapter.

Penny Abeywardena, "A Carnivore's Case for Veganism," *Forbes*, November 22, 2023. https://www.forbes.com/sites/pennyabeywardena/2023/11/22/a-carnivores-case-for-veganism/.

Gary L Francione and Anna E Charlton, "The Case Against Pets," Aeon, 8 September 2016. https://aeon.co/essays/why-keeping-a-pet-is-fundamentally-unethical.

Hailey Huget, "How the Animal Rights Movement Hurts Its Own Cause," *Current Affairs*, April 2021. https://www.currentaffairs.org/news/2021/04/how-the-animal-rights-movement-hurts-its-own-cause.

Jack McCordick, "Why Wild Animals Should Have Property Rights," Yale Law School, February 11, 2021. https://law.yale.edu/yls-today/news/why-wild-animals-should-have-property-rights.

Martha Nussbaum, "They Can Think, Feel Pain, Love. Isn't It Time Animals Had Rights?" *Harvard Gazette*, January 24, 2023. https://news.harvard.edu/gazette/story/2023/01/they-can-think-feel-pain-love-isnt-it-time-animals-had-rights/.

Kelsey Piper, "The Animal Rights Movement Was Once Locked in Bitter Debate. Now It's Getting Things Done," Vox, August 9, 2024. https://www.vox.com/future-perfect/365147/animal-welfare-factory-farming-effective-altruism-activism.

Michael Pollan, "An Animal's Place," *New York Times,* November 10, 2002. https://www.nytimes.com/2002/11/10/magazine/an-animal-s-place.html.

Benjamin Selwyn and Charis Davis, "The Case for Socialist Veganism," *Monthly Review*, February 1, 2024. https://monthlyreview.org/2024/02/01/the-case-for-socialist-veganism/.

Kelefa Sanneh, "How Far Should We Carry the Logic of the Animal-Rights Movement?" *The New Yorker,* April 29, 2024. https://www.newyorker.com/magazine/2024/05/06/how-far-should-we-carry-the-logic-of-the-animal-rights-movement.

Saskia Stucki, "Ethical and Practical Arguments for Animal Rights," *Politics and Rights Review*, April 24, 2025. https://politicsrights.com/ethical-practical-arguments-animal-rights/.

OPPOSING VIEWPOINTS® SERIES

Chapter 2

Do Nonhuman Animals Have Rights?

Chapter Preface

Now that we've had a look at the state of animal rights around the world and learned something of the history of the animal rights movement, we dig into the basic issue. Do nonhuman animals have rights at all?

As we saw in the previous chapter, there is a difference between animal welfare and animal rights. Most people agree that it is important to consider the welfare of animals, even though people can disagree in good faith about the details of what constitutes animal welfare and what humans should be expected to do to ensure that welfare.

Rights are another matter. To give animals rights in the legal sense would mean an animal—or a human on behalf of that animal—could sue in court if those rights are violated. To many that seems a little weird. But not to philosopher Martha Nussbaum. One of the authors here interviews her about her views.

Another author points out that though we have made great strides in the area of animal rights, we still exclude a lot of animals from the protections that are in place—farm animals and animals grown for food, for example.

One of the most basic rights is the right to be free from pain. Though it is clear that animals can experience sensations that we would identify as pain if *we* felt them, that's not so clear with animals. One author here argues that there is a difference between experiencing something that makes you wince and pull away, for example, and actually suffering. In order to justify granting animals the right to be free from pain, we would need to show that they are capable not just of feeling pain, but of suffering.

If we are to grant the right of animals to be free from pain, then we must know they can experience pain. In order to enforce laws that forbid inflicting pain on animals, we must be able to measure that pain. The authors of the first viewpoint in this chapter discuss how that objective can be achieved.

Viewpoint 1

> *"We know that animals certainly feel physical pain, but what is less clear is whether this emotional suffering that we feel can be said to be true of animals."*

To Address Animals' Pain, We Must Be Able to Measure It

Andrea Nolan

One of the arguments in favor of animal rights is that animals feel pain—but do they? In this viewpoint, the author explores that question and marks the distinction between the experience of pain and the experience of suffering. She also explains why we must be able to measure pain if we are to manage it. Andrea Nolan is principal and vice-chancellor of Edinburgh Napier University and a member of the World Small Animal Global Pain Council.

As you read, consider the following questions:

1. What are some of the "pain behaviors" described in this essay?
2. Why might animals actually suffer more from their pain than do humans, according to Nolan?
3. What is the Glasgow Composite Pain Scale?

Pain is a complex experience involving sensory and emotional components: it is not just about how it feels, but also how it makes you feel. And it is these unpleasant feelings that cause the suffering we humans associate with pain.

The science of suffering is well documented in the book of the same name by Patrick Wall. We know that animals certainly feel physical pain, but what is less clear is whether this emotional suffering that we feel can be said to be true of animals. And if it is, how we go about measuring it.

As a subjective emotion, pain can be experienced even in the absence of physical tissue damage, and the level of feeling can be modified by other emotions including fear, memory and stress. Pain also has different dimensions—it is often described in terms of intensity but it also has "character", for example the pain of a pin-prick is very different from that of a toothache, a slipped disc or labour pain. Nearly all of us have experienced pain in our lives, but for each person, the experience is uniquely individual.

To understand or appreciate others' pain we mostly rely on what they report. But there are many who either cannot communicate their pain verbally, babies for example, or effectively, like those with dementia or learning disabilities. In these situations, others must use a range of factors to judge the presence of pain and its impact on the individual.

Pain is not all bad—it serves a protective function, to keep us away from further danger, to help us heal, for example by stopping us from putting weight on a sprained ankle. But if it isn't managed effectively it can have a major negative impact on our lives inducing fear, anger, anxiety or depression – all emotions which may in turn exacerbate it. And chronic pain is a major concern to millions of individuals and to our societies around the world.

Pain in Animals

The nature of pain is perhaps even more complex in animals. How pain is sensed and the physical processes behind this are remarkably similar and well conserved across mammals and humans. There are also many similarities in pain behaviours across the species, for example they may stop socialising with people and/or other animals, they may eat less, they may vocalise more and their heart rate may rise. The capacity of animals to suffer as sentient creatures is well established and enshrined in law in many countries, however we don't understand well how they actually experience pain.

Some aspects of the experience and expression of pain are not likely to be the same as in humans. First, animals cannot verbally communicate their pain. Dogs may yelp and you may notice behaviour change but what about your pet rabbit, cat, tortoise or horse? Animals rely on human observers to recognise pain and to evaluate its severity and impact. Without the ability to understand soothing words that explain that following surgery to repair a bone fracture, their pain will be managed (hopefully) and will subside, animals may also suffer more when in pain than we do.

The debate around animals' capacity to experience pain and suffer raged in the 20th century, but as we developed a greater understanding of pain, and studied its impact on the aspects of animal life that we could measure, we veterinary surgeons, along with many behavioural and animal scientists, recognised the significant impact of untreated pain, and we now believe this experience causes them to suffer.

For example, we know that animals and indeed birds with clinical signs of pain (limping) will choose to eat food containing pain-killing drugs (analgesics) over untreated food, and by measures of behaviour, they will improve.

Similarly many studies in a range of domestic animals have indicated that animals who have had surgery but not had adequate pain relief demonstrate behaviours reflective of pain which are alleviated when they are treated with analgesics such as morphine.

We also know that it is not just our dogs and cats that can suffer pain—there is an equally strong evidence base for the presence and negative impact of pain in sheep, cattle, pigs and horses among other species. But recognising pain in these different species is part of the complexity associated with animal pain. Managing it in animals that we rear for food and those that we keep as companions is equally challenging.

Behavioural disturbances have long been recognised as potential indicators of the presence of pain in animals. However it is important to recognise that each species manifests its own sometimes unique pain-related behaviours or behavioural disturbances in different ways, often rooted in the evolutionary process, so prey species, for example, are less likely to "advertise" an increased vulnerability to predators. Dogs may become aggressive, or quiet, or may stop socialising with "their" humans and other dogs. Sheep, on the other hand, may appear largely the same when casually observed.

Some expressions of pain however may be conserved. A recent paper suggested commonality in some features of facial expression during acute pain experiences in several animal species and humans.

These findings and much other work are being incorporated into tools to evaluate animal pain, because in the words of Lord Kelvin, the great Glaswegian scientist behind the Kelvin temperature scale, said: "When you cannot measure it, when you cannot express it in number … you have scarcely, in your thoughts, advanced to the stage of science, whatever the matter may be".

So in order to treat and manage pain effectively we must measure it.

And there is a huge demand for these tools. The Glasgow Composite Pain Scale, a simple tool to measure acute pain in dogs and first published in 2007, has been translated into six languages. It is used in veterinary practices to measure pain to treat it effectively. It has also been used to evaluate the effectiveness of new analgesic drugs that are being developed by animal health companies. Tools to measure the impact of chronic pain, such as osteoarthritis, on the quality of life of dogs are now available and are a significant advance in managing chronic conditions.

There is now a global effort to raise awareness of pain in animals. Recently the World Small Animal Veterinary Association launched the Global Pain Council and published a treatise for vets and animal keepers worldwide to promote pain recognition, measurement and treatment. Dogs may be man's best friend, but for all those who work with, care for and enjoy the company of animals, understanding how their pain feels is essential to improving the quality of their lives.

Viewpoint 2

"Animals need freedom from pain. Absolutely. But they also need sociability with creatures of their own kind. They need stimulation of their senses. They need to have a diverse sensory environment. ... And they need to have room to move around."

Animals Should Have Their Rights Defended in Court

Hope Reese

In this article, Hope Reese interviews philosopher Martha Nussbaum about her then-new book, which takes an extreme view of animal rights. Reese is a journalist based in Budapest, Hungary. She writes for the New York Times, the Atlantic, Vox, and many other publications.

As you read, consider the following questions:

1. What is the "capabilities approach" to animal rights as described here?
2. What is the danger of using the "so-like-us" approach to granting animal rights, according to Nussbaum?
3. How does Nussbaum describe sentience?

Should a hummingbird be able to be a plaintiff in court? According to philosopher Martha Nussbaum, the answer is yes.

In her new book, *Justice for Animals: Our Collective Responsibility,* the distinguished professor of law and philosophy at the University of Chicago offers a new theory of animal justice that is meant to inform our law and policy. Her theory is based on the "capabilities approach," which looks not only at the harm done to animals, but whether we're infringing on their freedom to live full lives.

Granting animals the rights, under the law, that they deserve has never been so urgent, Nussbaum contends.

Animals are being threatened as a direct result of human activity. "The habitats of large land animals are shrinking. In the seas, plastic trash is choking whales and dolphins," she says. "Oil drilling is polluting the sea with [damaging] noise. And in the skies, air pollution is choking migratory birds."

"Human domination is doing a lot of harm," says Nussbaum. "We need to forge a human consensus to do something about the problem."

Nussbaum hopes her theory could be integrated into a "virtual constitution," adopted across the globe. She believes that the most egregious offenses—factory farming, puppy mills—should be the first we shut down.

I talked with Nussbaum about how we should think about animal rights and how laws might change to allow animals to live peacefully and freely. Here is our conversation, edited for clarity.

Hope Reese: Why now, more than at any point in history, should we consider animal rights?

Martha Nussbaum: Science has made enormous progress in the last 30 years. It's clear that animals are not brute beasts; they have complicated forms of perception, some of which humans don't even have. There's a lot of evidence that animals have complicated behaviors—social behaviors that are learned, not just genetic. They are like humans—they develop their behaviors through learning.

Thirty years ago, people thought birds had no intelligence at all. They thought, "Oh, if you don't have a neocortex, you don't have any intelligence." But birds, by a different evolutionary path, have converged on a lot of the abilities that humans and other mammals get through the neocortex. And they're some of the most intelligent creatures. They communicate in languages that even involve syntax. They do wonderful feats of social interaction. They're also really resourceful in the way they plan ahead. Birds can navigate by sensing magnetic fields. That's something that humans can't do.

HR: Why is it important that animals have social learning?

MN: The key behaviors of marine mammals are learned through social teaching. They're not automatons; they're much more like humans than we thought. It tells us what harm we do when we rip their social fabric apart. When we kidnap young whales and put them in a theme park, this deprives them of the chance to learn to be a whale or a dolphin—just as a human being who's brought up without any human company would be deformed beyond recognition.

HR: What kind of animals should be granted justice, in your view?

MN: It's important to ask which animals are sentient—that is, capable not only of feeling pain, but of having a point of view of the world. Right now we believe that vertebrates and many invertebrates have those capacities. Scientists think the crustaceans probably don't and that insects probably don't. It's important to develop ethical criteria, but then to be prepared to use them in accordance with what we know.

HR: What is the difference between your theory and others? Why do you think yours is better?

MN: The Nonhuman Rights Project does a lot of litigation on behalf of animals, using what I call the "so-like-us" approach—which judges animals by an alleged likeness to human beings, using the old traditional idea of a ladder of nature with us securely at the top. It's a religious idea, which means we're closer to God and the others straggle behind.

Steven Wise uses this approach because he thinks he'll be able to make progress on behalf of animals such as elephants, that he judges to be very human. But if you use the wrong approach, it sends you down the wrong path. It means that these animals are cut off legally and morally from the other animals who are suffering greatly, and who are very intelligent in their own way. It also presents a false picture of nature. There is no vertical ranking of creatures—each has their own idiosyncrasies, their own abilities. What we really should be doing is relating to each creature in its own way.

The utilitarian view of Jeremy Bentham and Principles of Morals and Legislation issued a clarion call for concern for animals. He pointed to the fact that animals are just as capable of suffering and dying as humans are. He thinks suffering is the key thing. The problem with that is, first of all, it's an average. It doesn't look at the world in terms of how each being gets to live. It asks: What is the average pleasure or the average pain? So it has trouble doing justice to those who are at the bottom of society's ladder.

Animals need freedom from pain. Absolutely. But they also need sociability with creatures of their own kind. They need stimulation of their senses. They need to have a diverse sensory environment, which they would seek out if they could. And they need to have room to move around. Elephants typically cover 200 miles a day. We need to know these things about creatures—and the utilitarian approach doesn't capture that.

The important thing is for each animal to have opportunities. I do think, over time, there can be convergence between these theories.

HR: What do animal rights currently look like, legally? You mention a case involving whale protection in your book.

MN: The U.S. Navy sonar program is now ruled illegal because it disrupts the behavior of whales. Well, the question was, what's bad? If you thought that only pain is bad, then you would think the sonar program is good because it does not inflict pain. But it does disrupt life activities. For example, interrupting reproduction, interrupting migration, creating heightened emotional stress.

This law that's been on the books for a very long time, the Marine Mammal Protection Act, was not held to create any problems for the U.S. Navy's sonar program. But when judges really looked at whales and looked at how they live and act, they realized that these disruptions caused an adverse impact.

HR: So you argue that the whales themselves should have the right to go to court as plaintiffs of a legal action, right?

MN: Standing means the ability to go to court as the plaintiff of an action. You have to show under the law of standing that you've suffered a particularized injury.

[Right now,] to challenge harm to animals, some human has to be able to go in and say, "I have suffered a particularized injury because of this abuse." And only certain kinds of injuries are admitted. But where are the animals?

Of course, animals don't walk into court themselves. But neither do most humans. We always have lawyers. Furthermore, there are lots of humans who have guardians: young children, people with severe cognitive disabilities, elderly people with severe cognitive disabilities, and so on. But those people, because they're human, have legal standing.

HR: Hypothetically, if animals are granted this right to defend themselves or have somebody defend them, how does that work?

MN: There are many humane organizations and NGOs trying to get into court representing animals. In the whale case, at least the Natural Resources Defense Council was allowed to go to court on behalf of the whales—that was a departure from previous practice. But that's always tricky and it requires judges who are sympathetic.

If the whales themselves would be the plaintiffs, then the NRDC would be their legal representative. There are many other organizations. The Humane Society of the United States does a lot of litigation on behalf of puppy mills. There's no shortage of qualified representatives. And the more local it is, the easier it is to do relief.

In Chicago, we have a Department of Child and Family Services where if I witness any abuse to a child on main campus, I am required as a mandatory reporter to call up the D.C. office and report that. I'm proposing something similar for animals. Of course, these things are covered by law, but the laws are not enforced. So the way we get enforcement is to have this mandatory reporting mechanism where people are required to call up the Department of Animal Welfare and report that I saw a dog being detained or I saw a dog that looks malnourished.

The Migratory Bird Treaty Act and the Marine Mammal Protection Act have been delegated to certain federal departments like the Department of Commerce. The thing is that their hands are tied—no one can really sue.

Inherent Value Does Not Grant Animals the Same Rights as Humans

In Tom Regan's book *The Case for Animal Rights,* he argues that all 'normal mammals over a year of age have the same basic moral rights' as humans. This basically means that the same ethical standards that apply to humans should apply to animals as well. Even though I feel animals and in particular mammals do deserve to have a level of ethical standards, putting them on same level as humans in my opinion is wrong. Regan uses the term inherent value to express why he feels this way, inherent value in the case of animal ethics can be described as the value an animal possesses in its own right, as an end-in-itself, the opposite of this is instrumental value which means that an animal only has a value to other animals such as human beings.

In Regan's argument he places a lot of importance on the distinction of mammals and other species making the argument that mammals are primarily the most important type of animal. In addition he says that the mammals have to be 'normal' and over one year old. I find all three of his statements slightly unjust. Firstly, what makes a mammal more special than a reptile or bird? Secondly, why does the animal have to be of a certain age to be classified to have a certain level of inherent value? I don't think there should be any correlation between age and inherent value especially if a theory states that there can be no middle ground in regards to inherent value. However one aspect of Regan's argument is that nonliving entities can have inherent values, largely because many of these nonsentient objects such as rocks and rivers have very important roles in an ecosystems, they can be habitats or can serve as protection for animals, making them crucial to the survival of the animals itself. All in all, I agree with some aspects Regan's explanation of animal's rights, however the main part of his theory that I do not agree with is the idea that a mammal either has or does not have inherited value. I feel that value differs from animal to animal and just because an animal has inherited value it shouldn't mean that they are allowed to have the same rights as humans.

"Animal Rights- Inherent Value" by Saahil Papar, Emory University.

If animals had standing, then those departments—in addition to some humane organizations—would be their legal representatives.

HR: This subject is personal to you—your daughter, Rachel, an animal rights lawyer, died in 2019. What did you learn, and how are you trying to carry on her work?

MN: As I was doing the work with Rachel earlier, I learned a lot through her about whales and dolphins—because that was her particular passion. That was the biggest surprise.

During the work on the book, I learned a lot more about farm animals, and pigs in particular. I really knew zero about birds. The pleasure of learning was so great—it didn't actually change the direction of my theory, but it made me think it's much more urgent.

VIEWPOINT 3

> *"[W]e have seen that the cited scientific evidence alone is silent on the question of whether fish feel pain, because it is silent on the question of whether fish are conscious."*

Reacting to Negative Stimuli Does Not Necessarily Mean an Animal Is Suffering

Alistair Robinson

In this viewpoint, the author considers the question of whether animals can suffer. He argues that while no one wants to see animals suffer, we need to give a lot of thought to what it means to experience pain, anxiety, and fear. Alistair Robinson is a software developer and civil engineering graduate with an interest in philosophy and science.

"Animal Rights, Anthropomorphism, and Traumatized Fish," by Alistair Robinson, *Philosophy Now*. Reprinted by permission.

As you read, consider the following questions:

1. How does Robinson distinguish between harmless and harmful anthropomorphism?
2. What are some differing ways of identifying suffering, as discussed here?
3. Why is consciousness important in any discussion of suffering?

Most of us are outraged by the violent actions of animal rights extremists, but at the same time the movement's ideas and assumptions are gaining a foothold in the media and the public imagination. From my own experience it seems that among young thinking people animal rights is a very attractive political and ethical stance. My question is this: how can we be sure that empathy for animals, concern for their moral status, and the desire to put them on a par with humans, do not stem only from a false attribution of uniquely human emotions?

We have a predisposition to see ourselves in the world around us: we endow the universe with human characteristics such as consciousness, and call it *God*; we hear an expression of love in a cat's purr; we see an ancient oak as dignified and venerable. This is anthropomorphism. We attribute human characteristics to the things of the world, and those things are independent of that attribution: the fact that we have decided that they have qualities of our own does not make a difference to the actuality of the things themselves. It is, though, natural and important to the way we perceive the world. Unfortunately this means that we often naturally perceive the world falsely. Now this is not always a problem: the dawn chorus sounds like joy, and it makes *us* joyful – so what? But there is an increasing acceptance of anthropomorphism in supposedly rational debates about the differences between humans and animals. And as we shall see, even in the scientific community there is a susceptibility to it.

Leaving aside the arguments about whether or not animals have, or *should* have, inalienable rights, one persuasive argument for better animal welfare is that the inhumane treatment of animals is uncivilized: that it dehumanizes and brutalizes us. After all, our actions are conscious and chosen, because we are uniquely self-aware and free. We can see that if cruelty repulses us and evokes imaginative emotions and empathy (anthropomorphic as we are) then it might follow that continually straining these responses will desensitize us to cruelty in general, stripping us of our compassion for *all* beings, including our fellow humans. And this may be true for society as well as for individuals.

Philosopher Daniel Dennett suggests that just as the mistreatment of the dead bodies of our loved ones would be unacceptable to us—despite our knowing that the *person* has gone—so there may be a similarly good reason to treat animals well, no matter if our empathy and compassion are anthropomorphic. We have beliefs and customs that are important to us, and not necessarily because they have obvious practical value or a basis in a true picture of the world.

I do believe that the humane treatment of animals is preferable for these reasons, but we need to distinguish between harmless and harmful anthropomorphism. Science is the part of society whose *raison d'être* is the establishment of a true picture of the world, and it cannot afford to relax about the encroachment of anthropomorphic fallacies. Some scientific results are now being claimed—often, it seems, by the scientists themselves—to bear out the assumptions of animal rights activists: 'Does a hook hurt a fish? The evidence is reeling in.'[1]

In this article I will concentrate on the concept of suffering. There are other fundamental problems to be tackled when looking deeply into animal rights philosophy: if we decide to give an animal independent moral status, doesn't that mean that we presuppose the capacity to make moral decisions, and ultimately the capacity of consciousness? Can a species be conscious at all if it has not developed language? Some neuroscientists, as well as some modern philosophers, have said that it cannot. And then we have the controversy over the communicative abilities of chimpanzees. I will look briefly at consciousness further on, but mostly I will leave these issues aside and concentrate on suffering.

Fish Trauma

A recent study by a team from the Roslin Institute and the University of Edinburgh concluded that fish feel pain, implying that angling is cruel. Researchers tested the neural responses of rainbow trout and injected the fish with mild poisons. A few incontrovertible statements can be made in the light of the study's findings: fish have specific neural receptors that respond to heat, mechanical pressure and acid; the neurons fire in a way very similar to the firing patterns of human neurons in response to adverse stimuli; fish behave abnormally when their lips are injected with bee venom and vinegar, rocking from side to side and breathing very rapidly; and the abnormal behaviours and symptoms are not seen—or at least not to the same extent—either in fish that are simply handled or those that are given an injection of a harmless substance.[2]

What are we to conclude from all this? The study is truly an addition to our knowledge—it is especially enlightening on the evolutionary divergence of bony fishes and cartilaginous fishes—but can we conclude from it that fish feel pain? To begin with there is the problem that such a conclusion depends upon a scientific definition of pain, of which there is none. We might define it with reference to the actions of neurons in response to adverse stimuli, but this is only the physiological cause: when we use the word we mean the *experience*. Even behavioural responses need not be concomitant with an experiential mental state. It seems to me that an adequate definition must take in psychology as well as physiology and behaviour. So it might be that we cannot proceed strictly by deduction from the scientific results to concluding that the fish are in pain. But why shouldn't we make a reasonable conclusion based on some other reasonable assumptions? It may seem too obvious to be denied that if another vertebrate species behaves in the same way as we do under a corresponding stimulus, and if its physiological responses to that stimulus are the same as ours, then it feels what we feel.

We can see the assumptions being made here more clearly if we consider a definition given by another contemporary philosopher, David DeGrazia, of another kind of suffering: anxiety. DeGrazia's definition gives four components to anxiety, all of which have been scientifically observed in animals:[3]

1. Autonomic hyperactivity (rapid pulse and breathing, sweating, etc.)

2. Motor tension (jumpiness)

3. Inhibition of normal behaviours

4. Hyperattentiveness (visual scanning, etc.)

These are the symptoms of anxiety that we see in humans. But it might be misleading to group these as a *definition* of anxiety, because we are accustomed to using the word to signify more than the physiological and behavioural symptoms. When we say anxiety and mean an experience, we presume the thing that allows us to experience in the first place: consciousness of the self existing through time, or *temporal self-awareness*. This is what allows us to be aware of what is happening to us. DeGrazia does in fact assume this to be the context of the four components, both in humans and in animals. So DeGrazia's definition of anxiety, if we are to apply it across the board, asks us to assume what we are trying to prove: that animals experience things in the way that we do. In other words, the term 'anxiety' comes preloaded with meanings that pertain to our subjective experiences and emotions—to the essence of being human. If you then strip down the meaning of the word so that it encompasses only behavioural and physiological effects you cannot get away with suggesting that the discovery of those effects in an animal implies all the other shades of meaning that you have already decided to strip away.

Pain and Suffering

I now want to suggest what I think may be the implicit logical argument of all those who claim there is scientific proof that animals experience something akin to human suffering; that fish feel pain or that deer suffer stress. But first I must clear up my meanings. In my argument so far, pain and anxiety are more or less interchangeable. We might also add fear to the list. They are kinds of suffering that have behavioural and physiological symptoms, and that are said by some to be experienced by animals. So to make things simpler I will use the word *suffering*. Now, I have cast doubt on certain uses of the words *pain* and *anxiety*. Taking this further (perhaps too far), even suffering could be said to apply only to humans. So for convenience I will use it to mean simply the state of a being subjected to adverse stimuli.

For the science to be conclusive on its own, the logic needs to run like this:

1. The nature of both human and non-human suffering is in essence physiological and behavioural.

2. The physiological and behavioural characteristics of suffering are the same in humans and non-humans.

3. Therefore non-human suffering is in essence the same as human suffering.

The logic is valid but not necessarily true: statement 2 is definitely provable but statement 1 is disputable. It could also be seen as an example of *petitio principii* reasoning, where the conclusion is taken for granted in a premise, in this case statement 1.

This is something of a caricature, and I did say earlier that even if a deductive argument doesn't work, we might still reasonably make conclusions. A fairer representation of the argument might be that the evidence points to the *probability* of pain and anxiety in animals, if we also accept that many animals are to some extent temporally self-aware, or conscious. Here we can see the same problem cropping up again: whatever the scientific results tell us, they need to be interpreted in a certain way if they are to lead to: QED fish feel pain. So the whole question turns on whether it is a reasonable assumption that animals are conscious, something that I cannot cover here in much depth. But crucially we have seen that the cited scientific evidence alone is silent on the question of whether fish feel pain, because it is silent on the question of whether fish are conscious.

Fish Brains

Suffering depends upon our sense of ourselves, our sense of the passage of time and of the changing fortunes in our lives. When we are subjected to adverse stimuli we feel pain, anxiety and fear for the very reason that we are conscious of what is happening to us—we *experience* the stimuli, not only respond automatically to them. But because we share so much of our evolutionary history with animals, the outward signs of these responses are similar. We recognize distress in another human being and can be forgiven for attributing the same set of emotions to an animal if we see it behave in the same way.

Even if we are looking only at the science we find disagreement. There is evidence that fish literally do not have the brains to experience pain. One expert in the field, James D. Rose, in his rebuttal to the claims of the Scottish researchers, seems understandably frustrated that they ignored his earlier work. Essentially his argument is that their research deals not with the conscious experience of pain, but only with unconscious responses to adverse stimuli, or *nociception*. Fish do not have an area of the brain corresponding to our own neural pain-processor—the neocortex—so that although the same signals are sent to the brain, there is no recognizable pain-experience-producing region to go to when they arrive. Fish do not have regions of the brain that produce the *unpleasantness* of pain. In humans these regions lie in the cerebral hemispheres, but fish have little more than a brainstem. This at the very least tells us that we cannot describe what it is like to be a 'suffering' fish, because its brain processes the signals in an alien way. How, then, can we make any sort of moral conclusion on this, unless we simply assume—guided by taste, inclination and sentiment—that fish do experience something like human suffering?[4]

Before I conclude, I will touch upon the problem of consciousness, which is probably the crux of the matter. I suggested earlier that a being cannot be conscious without language. Neuroscientists Gerald M. Edelman and Giulio Tononi have written that the concepts of the self and the past and future emerged only when language appeared in the course of evolution, in communities of speakers. There must have been an intimate connection between social development and the evolution of consciousness, and language must be the likeliest contender for that connection.

It has been argued that although we (a) use language and (b) are conscious, (b) need not depend on (a). If it did, the argument goes, babies would not be able to feel pain or experience fear before they developed their language ability. There are two points to be made here. First, it is probably true that newborn babies are not quite conscious. We nurture and protect them while knowing that from the outset they are *developing*, becoming more and more human. Second, modern cognitive psychology and linguistics tells us that a baby is learning language right from the start. Newborn babies have linguistic skills, because language is partly built-in: it is not just a matter of filling an empty brain with vocabulary and syntax. It seems problematic, then, to back up the claim that language is not necessary for consciousness by comparing animals to babies, which are just humans in development.

Conclusion

Few of us want to see animals being treated inhumanely, but we would do well to consider how our natural and perhaps inaccurate assumptions about the inner lives of animals can affect our understanding of the true differences between ourselves and other species. The notion of animal rights has more adherents than ever before, and many who profess no passionate beliefs on the subject seem to accept its validity. The media is currently highly responsive to claims about pain and stress in animals, and science at times is taking anthropomorphism at face value, and allowing it to bias its conclusions. This could be to do with the mood of the age, one that happily brings man down a peg or two on the scale of importance at every opportunity. While it is to be welcomed that thanks to science we no longer see ourselves at the centre of the universe as destiny's chosen creatures, we also need to keep ourselves from allowing the spirit of the times to colour our unique, rational understanding of the world.

References

1. J. Randerson, *New Scientist*, May 15, 2003

2. Sneddon, Braithwaite and Gentle, 'Do fish have nociceptors: Evidence for the evolution of a vertebrate sensory system', *Proceedings of the Royal Society* 2003

3. David DeGrazia, *Animal Rights: A Very Short Introduction* (Oxford University Press 2002)

4. See two papers by James D. Rose available online: 'Do Fish Feel Pain?' (http://www.cotrout.org/do_fish_feel_pain.htm) and a rebuttal to Sneddon, Braithwaite and Gentle's paper at the website of the European Anglers Alliance, http://www.eaa-europe.org/2003/PFCasework/FishPain-Rebuttal-JamesRose-EN.htm.

Viewpoint 4

> *"Changing public opinion and subsequent behaviours is the bedrock upon which campaigns for the rights of animals are built."*

Despite Advances, Animals Continue to Suffer

Dave Neale

This article was written on the occasion of International Animal Rights Day. It celebrates advances in animal rights, but urges readers to think about those animals that we have not included in laws that protect other animals. Dave Neale is the animal welfare Director of Animals Asia.

As you read, consider the following questions:

1. How has public opinion changed about animals in recent years?
2. What examples does Neale give that illustrate our contradictory notions about animal rights?
3. Despite advances in humane treatment of animals, what do we still need to be thinking about, according to this author?

In a world where animal use has become so central to our daily lives, is it possible for society to question societal norms and grant animals with rights similar to those that in general we agree are applicable to all humans?

Rights are defined as 'legal, social, or ethical principles of freedom or entitlement…' The process of establishing rights for people continues to be a long term battle with many wins along the way but still there is much work to do to ensure that all people have the same rights.

It is safe to assume that most people will agree that all humans are entitled to equal human rights, despite many supporting practices that fundamentally impact on the rights of others. It is not so safe to assume that most people support the case for all animals to be entitled to equal rights, in fact the case for animals is often very unclear with legal, social and ethical differences existing between and within species.

The UK's Animal Welfare Act (AWA) 2006 defines 'animal' as 'a vertebrate other than man', but adds that invertebrates could be brought within the scope of the Act 'if the appropriate national authority is satisfied, on the basis of scientific evidence, that animals of the kind concerned are capable of experiencing pain or suffering' (s1(4)). In Nov 2021 the UK government extended the scope of the Animal Welfare (Sentience) Bill to recognise lobsters, octopus, crabs and all other decapod crustaceans and cephalopod molluscs as sentient beings. to recognise lobsters, octopus, crabs and all other decapod crustaceans and cephalopod molluscs as sentient beings.

Whilst this is one of the most advanced pieces of global legislation for animals it still does not include millions of animal species from groups such as the insects, spiders, centipedes and millipedes, despite a growing body of research suggesting many such animals are capable of experiencing pain and anxiety leading to suffering.

Despite legislation such as the AWA being in place for all vertebrates, society continues to support/tolerate activities that actively cause certain species unnecessary suffering. The AWA is, arguably, relevant for animals such as grouse and fish that have been under human care and released into human-managed environments, yet grouse shooting and recreational fishing persist. Society is much less likely to tolerate such activities if we were to breed dogs or dolphins to be released into the wild to be hunted and killed in the same way.

In another example, society actively encourages the breeding, raising, transportation and slaughter of animals such as hens, pigs, cows, turkeys etc. for consumption. These animals are protected by the AWA yet many millions suffer miserable lives on intensive farms. Practices that once again it is highly unlikely we would tolerate if animals such as chimpanzees or elephants were being farmed for us to eat.

At the species level, rabbits (for example) straddle a number of differing legal and ethical positions. One rabbit may occupy a place in a loving home and be legally protected from harm as a companion animal, a second rabbit may occupy a place in a research laboratory where it has been deemed necessary to perform certain experiments upon them, even though they may cause some degree of suffering.

A third may be caged on an intensive farm being fattened for slaughter with minimal legal protections in place to ensure they do not suffer, and a fourth may suffer in the wild as they are deemed as a 'pest' and the law allows the extermination of pest species with no consideration to their individual welfare.

These examples represent clear social and ethical differences in the value that we assign to both different species and individuals within the same species, and subsequently different species and individuals being afforded greater and lesser protection despite all being covered within the law.

The values that we as individuals assign to animals, in general, reflect the society in which we have grown up within. If we grow up in a society where the suffering of animals within intensive farms or for our entertainment is deemed necessary then it is likely that these views will persist across the generations. But simply because current societal views support such acts this does not make them the right thing to do.

Changing public opinion and subsequent behaviours is the bedrock upon which campaigns for the rights of animals are built upon.

Scientific discoveries first in anatomy, then evolutionary theory, and most recently in animal behaviour and cognition have developed our understanding of animals as socially, emotionally and cognitively complex individuals, sentient beings able to feel pain and with the capacity to suffer, and this understanding has led to our increasing concern for their welfare.

This in turn has led to subsequent political advancements with legislation protecting animals now existing within countries across the world. Yet despite these major advancements billions of animals continue to suffer due to our unequal treatment of them at the species and intraspecies level.

International Animal Rights Day provides us with an opportunity to reflect on our own values towards both the animals that we interact with and those we impact upon via our daily behaviours and choices. A chance to think about the complex emotional and cognitive lives of so many other animals that have not as yet been granted the same societal, ethical and in many cases the legal rights that we have given to animals such as our companion animals living in our homes. And a chance for us to change our behaviours to help to address this imbalance.

Periodical and Internet Sources Bibliography

The following articles have been selected to supplement the diverse views presented in this chapter.

Emma Atkinson, "The Right to Personhood: One Professor's Fight for Animals," University of Denver, February 18, 2025. https://www.du.edu/news/right-personhood-one-professors-fight-animals.

Mary Bates, "A Test for Animal Consciousness," *Psychology Today*, May 27, 2021. https://www.psychologytoday.com/us/blog/animal-minds/202105/a-test-for-animal-consciousness.

Susan Blackmore, "Are Humans the Only Conscious Animal?" *Scientific American,* September 1, 2018. https://www.scientificamerican.com/article/are-humans-the-only-conscious-animal/.

Pablo P. Castello, "Is Seeing Believing? Not Really, so Animal Welfare Campaigns Should Take a Different Approach," *The Conversation*, June 3, 2024. https://theconversation.com/is-seeing-believing-not-really-so-animal-welfare-campaigns-should-take-a-different-approach-230731.

Jan Dutkiewicz, "You're Wrong about PETA," Vox, August 8, 2024. https://www.vox.com/future-perfect/364284/peta-protests-animal-rights-factory-farming-effective.

David Favre, JD, "Should Nonhuman Animals Be Recognized Legally as Persons?" *American Medical Association Journal of Ethics*, September 2024. https://journalofethics.ama-assn.org/article/should-nonhuman-animals-be-recognized-legally-persons/2024-09.

Avery Hurt, "Do Fish Feel Pain?," *Discover*, November 7, 2023, updated March 25, 2024. https://www.discovermagazine.com/planet-earth/do-fish-feel-pain.

Rona Johnson,"What's Up with Animal Rights Activists?," *The Fence Post*, April 26, 2024. https://www.thefencepost.com/news/whats-up-with-animal-rights-activists/.

Michael Marshall, "This Look at Animal Consciousness Is a Moral Workout—in the Best Way," *New Scientist*, 29 January 2025. . https://www.newscientist.com/article/mg26535284-100-this-look-at-animal-consciousness-is-a-moral-workout-in-the-best-way/.

Petra Stock, “Do Fish Have Feelings? Scientists Believe They’re Getting Closer to an Answer,” *The Guardian*, 14 September 2024. https://www.theguardian.com/environment/2024/sep/14/do-fish-have-feelings-sydney-university-research-project.

OPPOSING VIEWPOINTS® SERIES

Chapter 3

Which Kinds of Nonhuman Animals Should Have Rights?

Chapter Preface

Few people would disagree with the idea that animals have emotions and can feel pain, that animals are conscious. Why would we keep pets if they weren't aware of themselves and of us? However, of all the many species in the world, which ones are conscious, and thus deserving of welfare protections and perhaps even legal rights? That's a much harder question to answer, but the authors in this chapter give it a go.

Some people have claimed that seeing consciousness in an animal is just a matter of anthropomorphism, or the tendency to see human traits in all living things (and oftentimes in the inanimate as well). However, it's likely not quite that simple. The authors here point to striking evidence that we should at least consider the possibility that many, even most, animals have some degree of sentience.

In the first viewpoint, the author argues that we need to give a great deal more thought to these questions. If invertebrates, for example, are sentient, then we need to consider their welfare, and we also need to consider what granting insects and spiders sentience would mean for humans.

Another author offers an overview of the history of animals right in India, and shows that even in this country with the one of the best traditions of being aware of animal rights, there is a still a long way to go to fully protect animals.

One author here grants full sentience to all animals and adds that it's just good practice to treat animals (and even teddy bears) as sentient, even if we aren't sure. Another viewpoint explores the way humans have a natural tendency to put things in categories and are determined to find a way to place humans in a category all by themselves. Exotic pets even get some room here, from a veterinarian who argues that wild animals should never be kept as pets.

VIEWPOINT 1

"The urge to attribute feelings to insects can be surprisingly strong."

We're Overlooking a Lot of Animals

Jonathan Birch

For some animals, it's easy to see that they are conscious, particularly dogs, cats, cows. However, what about insects? Here, the author argues that we need to think more carefully about how we decide which animals deserve protection. Jonathan Birch is an associate professor of philosophy at the London School of Economics and principal investigator on the Foundations of Animal Sentience project.

"Which Animals Should Be Considered Sentient in the Eyes of the Law?," by Jonathan Birch, *Guardian*, May 16, 2021. Reprinted by permission.

As you read, consider the following questions:

1. Why, according to Birch, are scientists divided on the issue of insect sentience?
2. What type of experiment convinced UK legislators to include octopuses in laws protecting animals?
3. What are some exceptions mentioned here to the protections offered even to mammals and fish?

Look a dog in the eye and a conscious being looks back. A being that feels hunger, thirst, warmth, cold, fear, comfort, pleasure, pain, joy. No one can seriously doubt this. The same is true of any mammal. You cannot watch rats playing hide and seek and doubt that they have feelings—that they are sentient creatures. But as animals become more distant from us in evolutionary terms, some doubt begins to creep in.

Consider a bee sneaking past the guards of a rival colony to steal honey. Or the Brazilian ants that, in order to hide their nest at the end of each day, seal off the entrance from the outside. Left out in the cold at night, these ants will never see the morning, but their sacrifice increases the chance that their sisters will. The urge to attribute feelings to insects can be surprisingly strong.

But then we think: wait, can we really talk like this? An insect's brain is organised completely differently from a mammal's. It is also much smaller (a bee has about 1m neurons, compared with our 100bn). Could insects be robot-like evolved machines with absolutely no experience or feeling? Or are we underestimating what a small brain can do?

New laws to impose some consistency in this area have been needed for a while. So the animal welfare (sentience) bill, introduced to parliament on Thursday, is a welcome development, as is the creation of an animal sentience committee. The bill includes vertebrates by default, but explicitly allows invertebrates to be added through statutory instruments. I can see the rationale for such an approach in an area where the science is moving quickly.

For instance, on the question of insect sentience, scientists are divided, partly because there has been no serious attempt to look for sentience in insects. The science at present is too uncertain to allow us to be confident one way or the other. I think that situation will change: one goal of my Foundations of Animal Sentience project is to address this.

If the evidence does point towards sentience being widespread among invertebrates, what then? Would we end up with absurd laws banning us from stepping on insects? No. Laws are limited by what is enforceable and reasonable. But think about insect farming, which currently falls outside the scope of animal welfare laws. Should it really be completely unregulated, or would some welfare regulations make sense? The question deserves careful thought.

Cases like these point to the need for a scientific approach to animal sentience: an approach that goes beyond our intuitive reactions, which are often anthropomorphic and mammal-centric. An approach based on looking at what feelings do for us, and then looking carefully for markers of analogous brain processes in other animals. Reflexes are not enough to establish sentience: it's important to show that the animal has a central system that values and disvalues stimuli. There is no single litmus test: many different markers are relevant. Insight can come from neuroscience, cognition, behaviour—and ideally all three pointing in the same direction.

One particular feeling has received a great deal of scientific attention: pain. That's partly because pain is a source of great ethical concern, and partly because scientists often want to use animals to understand human pain.

For instance, there is a setup called a "conditioned place preference" test that is designed to test for enduring pain. In the original test, rats choose between three chambers. At first, they have no preference. But then, some are injured and are placed in one chamber. Then they are given painkillers and placed in a different chamber. The question is: will the rats develop a lasting aversion to the chamber where they experienced the injury, and a lasting preference for the chamber where they experienced the effects of painkillers when injured? They do, unsurprisingly. They are mammals like us, after all.

In a striking recent experiment, octopus expert Robyn Crook tried the same type of test on octopuses—and they passed too. Octopuses learned to avoid a chamber where they experienced a noxious stimulus (acetic acid on the skin) and learned to prefer a chamber where they could experience a local anaesthetic on the affected area.

Evidence of this general type convinced UK legislators in 1993 to bring octopuses within the scope of laws on animal experimentation. In 2010, this was extended throughout the EU to all cephalopod molluscs, including squid and cuttlefish. We now have an odd situation: the welfare of cephalopods is protected in science but nowhere else. Given this, the government's plan to "consider further protections" for cephalopods and decapod crustaceans (such as crabs and lobsters), where supported by evidence, is welcome.

Of course, the sentience bill will not solve any animal welfare problem by itself. Pigs, chickens and fish are widely considered sentient already. Yet pregnant sows are still often kept in farrowing crates, unable to turn around. Chickens are often raised in sheds with space equivalent to about one A4 sheet of paper for each bird. Fish are included in the Animal Welfare Act, but anything that occurs "in the normal course of fishing" is exempt from that act.

The knowledge that humans recognise them as sentient would come as small comfort to these animals. The burden still falls on us as individual consumers to oppose questionable practices. We should respect all sentient life and try to set the boundaries of the law in line with current science. This captures something important about our shared values. We shouldn't be afraid of following the evidence, wherever it may lead.

Viewpoint 2

> *"Protection of animals is enshrined as a fundamental duty in the Indian Constitution."*

India Law Almost Gets It Right

Taruni Kavuri

As we saw in Chapter One, a cultural respect for animals goes back thousands of years in India. Unsurprisingly, today the country has some of the world's most robust animal welfare protections. In this viewpoint, the author takes a look at the current state of animal welfare laws in India. Taruni Kavuri is a corporate lawyer in Mumbai, Maharashtra, India.

"Overview of Animal Laws in India," by Taruni Kavuri, Michigan State University College of Law. Reprinted by permission.

As you read, consider the following questions:

1. How have India's animal protection laws changed over the years?
2. How did the 1960 Prevention of Cruelty to Animals Act define "animal"? What exceptions did it make?
3. What does Kavuri mean when she says constitutional protections are principles rather than laws enforceable in court?

Introduction

India, the seventh largest country in the world, is one of the most bio-diverse regions of the world containing four of the world's 36 biodiversity hotspots. It is home to animals ranging from the Bengal Tigers to the Great Indian Rhinoceros and animal protection and welfare in in the country has taken a prominent position over the recent years. Protection of animals is enshrined as a fundamental duty in the Indian Constitution and there exist several animal welfare legislations in India such as the Prevention of Cruelty to Animals Act 1960 and the Wildlife Protection Act 1972 at the Central level and cattle protection and cow slaughter prohibition legislations at the State levels.

The Indian Penal Code (IPC) 1860 is the official criminal code of India which covers all substantive aspects of criminal law. Section 428 and 429 of the IPC provides for punishment of all acts of cruelty such as killing, poisoning, maiming or rendering useless of animals. The aforementioned legislations have been enacted to obviate unnecessary pain and suffering of animals and similar legislations continue to be enacted according to changing circumstances. Notwithstanding specific statutes, further protections for animals lie under general concepts such as tort law, constitutional law, etc.

The Constitution of India 1960

The Constitution of India 1960 makes it the "duty of every citizen of India to protect and improve the natural environment, including forests, lakes, rivers and wildlife, and to have compassion for all living creatures." This Constitutional duty of animal protection is supplemented by the Directive Principle of State Policy under Article 48A that:

> *The State shall endeavor to protect and improve the environment and to safeguard the forests and wildlife of the country.*

Both the above constitutional provisions were introduced by the 42nd Amendment in 1976. While they are not directly enforceable in Indian courts, they lay down the groundwork for legislations, policies and state directives in furtherance of animal protection at the Central and State levels. Moreover, they may be enforced in courts by taking an expansive judicial interpretation and bringing them within the ambit of the fundamental Right to Life and Liberty under Article 21 which is judicially enforceable.

Sources of Law

The primary sources of law in India are the Constitution, statutes (legislations), customary law and case laws. India is a federal union divided into 28 States and 8 Union Territories. The respective States are administered by their own State governments while the Union Territories are federal territories directly governed by the central Government of India. The Parliament of India is the supreme legislative body of the country while Indian States have their respective State Legislatures. Statutes are enacted by the Parliament for the entire country, by the State legislatures for respective States and by the Union Territory legislatures for respective Union Territories. Central laws enacted by the Parliament can be checked and controlled only by the Constitution of India. State laws may be overridden.

In addition to these primary legislations, there also exists a vast body of subordinate legislation like rules, regulations and by-laws enacted by Central/State governments and local authorities such as municipal corporations and *gram panchayats* (local village bodies). Given the separation of powers in India between the Legislature, Executive and Judiciary branches of government, the three branches are vested with different functions. While the primary responsibility of drafting legislations lies with the legislature, sometimes the responsibility is given to the Executive branch in order to draft legislations known as delegated legislation.

India follows the common law system based on recorded judicial precedents handed down by the British colony. Therefore, it places significant reliance on precedents and case laws in the development of law and jurisprudence. Judicial decisions of higher courts such as the Supreme Court of India and High Courts of different States carry significant legal weight and are binding on lower courts.

India is a land of wide religious and cultural diversity. Therefore, some personal laws, local customs, religious texts and conventions which are not against statute, morality, public policy and larger social welfare are also recognized to have a legal character and are taken into account by courts in the administration of justice.

Allocation of Powers between the Centre and the States

Article 245 of the Indian Constitution holds that subject to the Constitution, the Indian Parliament can make laws for the whole or part of territory of India. Territory of India includes States, Union Territories and other territories such as enclaves within India.

Article 246 lays down the subject-matter of laws made by the Parliament and the State Legislatures. This subject-matter is allocated into three lists contained in the Seventh Schedule:

- The Union List: the Parliament has exclusive power to make laws with respect to the matters enumerated within this list.
- The State List: State Legislatures have the exclusive power to make laws with respect to the matters enumerated within this list.
- Concurrent List: both the Parliament and State Legislatures have the power to make laws with respect to the matters enumerated within this list.

In the context of animal rights, the following matters have been allocated in the State and Concurrent List.

Item 14 of the State List provides that the States have the power to "[p]reserve, protect and improve stock and prevent animal diseases and enforce veterinary training and practice."

In the Concurrent List, both the Centre and the States have the power to legislate on:

- Item 17: "Prevention of cruelty to animals."
- Item 17B: "Protection of wild animals and birds."

The Prevention of Cruelty to Animals Act, 1960

The basic cruelty law of India is contained in the Prevention of Cruelty to Animals Act 1960. The objective of the Act is to prevent the infliction of unnecessary pain or suffering on animals and to amend the laws relating to the prevention of cruelty to animals. The Act defines "animal" as any living creature other than a human being.

In accordance with Chapter II of the Act, the Government of India established the Animal Welfare Board of India (AWBI) with some of the following functions:

- Advising the central government regarding amendments and rules to prevent unnecessary pain while transporting animals, performing experiments on animals or storing animals in captivity.
- Encouragement of financial assistance, rescue homes and animal shelters for old animals.
- Advising the government on medical care and regulations for animal hospitals.
- Imparting education and awareness on humane treatment of animals.
- Advising the central government regarding general matters of animal welfare.

The Act enumerates different variants of cruelty to animals under Section 11 as the following actions:

a) Beating, kicking, overriding, overloading, torturing and causing unnecessary pain to any animal.
b) Using an old or injured or unfit animal for work (the punishment applies to the owner as well as the user).
c) Administering an injurious drug/medicine to any animal.
d) Carrying an animal in any vehicle in a way that causes it pain and discomfort.
e) Keeping any animal in a cage where it doesn't have reasonable opportunity of movement.
f) Keeping an animal on an unreasonably heavy or short chain for an unreasonable period of time.
g) Keeping an animal in total and habitual confinement with no reasonable opportunity to exercise.
h) Being an owner failing to provide the animal with sufficient food, drink or shelter.
i) Abandoning an animal without reasonable cause.

j) Willfully permitting an owned animal to roam on streets or leaving it on the streets to die of disease, old age or disability.
k) Offering for sale an animal which is suffering pain due to mutilation, starvation, thirst, overcrowding or other ill-treatment.
l) Mutilating or killing animals through cruel manners such as using strychnine injections.
m) Using an animal as bait for another animal solely for entertainment.
n) Organizing, keeping, using or managing any place for animal fighting.
o) Shooting an animal when it is released from captivity for such purpose.

However, the Act does not consider as cruelty the dehorning/castration of cattle in the prescribed manner, destruction of stray dogs in lethal chambers in prescribed manner and extermination of any animal under the authority of law. This Section provides somewhat of a leeway.

Part IV of the Act covers experimentation of animals. The Act does not render unlawful experimentation on animals for the purpose of advancement by new discovery of physiological knowledge or knowledge to combat disease, whether of human beings, animals or plants. It envisages the creation of a committee for control and supervision of experiments on animals by the central government which even has the power to prohibit experimentation if so required.

Chapter V covers the area of performing animals. Section 22 prohibits exhibiting or training an animal without registration with the AWBI. The Section prohibits animals such as monkeys, bears, lions, tigers, panthers and bulls from being utilized as performing animals.

Animal Sentience in Insects and Worms?

An article in *Undark* magazine has asked whether invertebrate animals, such as fruit flies, bees or nematode worms, experience pain and should receive some protection under animal welfare laws.

The author, Katya Zimmer, looked at the latest studies and asked scientists for their opinions.

While none of those asked thought research on invertebrate species should stop, some scientists believed species with relatively simple brains, like insects, or perhaps even those with no central nervous system at all, deserve ethical consideration.

Asked by *Undark* about the issue of sentience, EARA executive director Kirk Leech said he was concerned that any further regulatory burden on researchers would only stifle scientific innovation.

Recently the UK Parliament passed an Animal Welfare (Sentience) Bill, which will require the Government to set up an Animal Sentience Committee to examine whether 'the welfare of animals as sentient beings' is considered in policy decisions.

Currently, only one country, Norway, regulates research on a species of insect—honeybees—and an article in *Science* has also highlighted research into whether bees feel pain.

"Animal sentience in insects and worms?" by Katya Zimmer, European Animal Research Association, August 08, 2022.

An additional leeway provided by the Act is that under Section 28, nothing contained in the Act shall render it an offence to kill any animal in a manner required by the *religion* of any community.

Considering the diversity of religions and traditions in India, this Section was considered imperative.

Treating animals cruelly is punishable with a fine of Rs. 10 which may extend to Rs. 50 on first conviction. On subsequent conviction within three years of a previous offence, it is punishable with a fine of Rs. 25 which may extend to Rs.

100 or imprisonment of three months or with both. Performing operations like Phooka or any other operations to improve lactation which is injurious to the health of the animal is punishable with a fine of Rs. 1000 or imprisonment up to 2 years or both. The government further has the power to forfeit or seize or destroy the animal. Contravention of any order of the committee regarding experimentation on animals is punishable with a fine up to Rs. 200.

Conclusion

The 42nd Amendment to the Indian Constitution in 1976 was a progressive step towards laying the groundwork for animal protection in India. The constitutional provisions establishing the duty of animal protection have resulted in the enactment of animal protection legislations both at the central and state level, most notable of which being the Prevention of Cruelty to Animals Act 1960. Furthermore, over the years Indian courts have developed a growing legal jurisprudence in animal law.

However, there is a still a long ways to go in truly developing a solid foundation for animal law in India. The provisions for animal protection in the Indian Constitution remain principles instead of concrete law enforceable in courts. The penalties under the Prevention of Cruelty to Animals Act 1960 for cruelty against animals are simply not strict enough to truly deter crimes against animals. The law is not strictly enforced and contains several provisions which provide leeway through which liability can be escaped. Extensive reforms need to take place in this regard to provide a stronger animal protection law for India.

Viewpoint 3

> *"Once life evolved the ability to move and become independent from photosynthesis, sentience inevitably evolved with it."*

Animals Are More Sentient Than You Think

Jordi Casamitjana

In this viewpoint, the author explores the concept of sentience, and argues that all animals are sentient, even ones that don't seem to be. Jordi Casamitjana is a zoologist and animal protector. He is the author of Ethical Vegan: A Personal and Political Journey to Change the World.

"Animals Are More Sentient Than You Think" by Jordi Casamitjana, March 5, 2021. This story was originally published by Sentient Media: https://sentientmedia.org/animals-are-more-sentient-than-you-think/. Reprinted by permission.

As you read, consider the following questions:

1. How does Casamitjana define "ethical vegan"?
2. How does he define "sentience"?
3. Why does Casamitjana greet his stuffed animals each day, even though he knows they can't hear him and are not aware of him?

"Hello, how're you doing?" This is what I often say to the small black teddy bear sitting on top of the pile of old letters by my London apartment's front door. I know she cannot hear me or understand me—she is not a sentient being—but I say it anyway. Why? Because this constantly reminds me that it is up to me to treat all sentient beings with respect, even those who may not understand human language. I am an ethical vegan, you see. I follow a philosophy based on avoiding harming any sentient being, and to be true to it I need to pay close attention to everything I do, and how I treat everyone around me.

What is sentience, anyway? This concept has been defined in many ways, and definitions change with culture. Some say that is the ability to feel "pain and pleasure," others say is the ability to experience "suffering and happiness," or "emotions and moods." Some may not accept all animals feel pain or suffering, claiming they need a sophisticated level of cognition or consciousness—they argue some animals they consider "inferior," such as worms and insects, are not sentient. I disagree with this anthropocentric view.

When I was writing my book *Ethical Vegan: A Personal and Political Journey to Change the World*, I spent some time researching the issue of sentience, and I finally arrived at my own definition:

> *At its most basic meaning, sentience is the ability to experience positive and negative sensations, which requires two things: firstly, senses to perceive the sensations from stimuli*

coming from the environment, and, secondly, a nervous system to process such sensations and translate them into experiences which allow the animals to react accordingly, depending on whether they are negative or positive (i.e. fleeing from an adverse environment or moving towards a source of food or a mate).

Sentient Earthlings

Concepts such as "feelings" are subjective, and therefore available only to the animal experiencing them, and we could never prove any organism (including a human) is sentient if we based it only on that. Fortunately, we do not need to know exactly what animals are feeling, but only whether they are experiencing something positive or negative, and the behavior of the animals can tell us that. Animals are sentient because they can behave in a way that means they can profit from the information sentience provide them. They can move away from something bad and get closer to something good. They can swallow something tasty and spit out something nasty.

They can feel, experience, and judge, and once they have judged, they can behave accordingly. We don't need to know exactly how they feel, what they experience, or how they reason. We only need to observe how they behave. This is how we know most animals are sentient, and that rocks, plants, and teddy bears are not. I am an ethologist (a zoologist specialized in animal behavior), and I have never seen any animal other than poriferans (aquatic sponges) behaving in such a way that suggests a lack of sentience.

Once life evolved the ability to move and become independent from photosynthesis, sentience inevitably evolved with it. Feeling pain is a particularly useful tool for avoiding injury and death, and the animal species whose members did not feel pain most likely became extinct. Equally, feeling comfort, pleasure, and even delight when finding maternal protection or succeeding in mating courtship will increase the chances of reaching a reproductive age—and once there, reproduce—which natural selection would favor. In fact, on planet Earth, with liquid water, a dynamic atmosphere, solid ground, and moving soil, sentience is likely to evolve independently all over the place. When you can dive to catch your dinner, fly to avoid winter, bask on a rock to catch the sun, or dig a hole to hide from predators, sentience is what you need. It makes sense, right?

It should be a no-brainer, but it is not. In a world where animal exploitation is heavily entrenched in most aspects of all human societies, commercial and cultural forces constantly work to deny the quality of sentience to non-human animals. Even when today's science clearly shows most animals are sentient, this denial is mainstream. Although all jurisdictions in developed countries accept all mammals and birds are sentient, and most also include the rest of the vertebrates (reptiles, amphibians, and fish), as far as invertebrates are concerned—who make up the majority of animals on this planet—there is much resistance.

However, in the last few years, there has been some progress. In various pioneering countries (such as New Zealand, Norway, Switzerland, Canada, and EU nations), some invertebrates are beginning to be accepted as sentient, and therefore are becoming legally protected like their vertebrate counterparts. In particular, cephalopods (a type of mollusk which includes octopus, cuttlefish, and squid) and decapods (a type of crustacean which includes crabs and lobsters).

What about the Tiny Animals?

With time, I hope more invertebrates will make it to the official list of protected sentient beings. Having studied social wasps for many years—who taught me many things about life and started me on my journey to veganism—I do not doubt that insects and arachnids are sentient too. Not an unexpected conclusion from a vegan zoologist, you may think. However, what is surprising is that within the "vegan" world—with its non-speciesist philosophy which predicates no animal species should be discriminated against—some people often referred to as ostrovegans eat bivalves (aquatic animals such as mussels, oysters, and clams characterized by having two shells that can close the animal in) because they don't consider them sentient. In my book I explain why I think they are wrong:

> *First of all, they are mollusks, and other mollusks have now been recognized as sentient beings. Second, they all have senses. In particular, all have mechanoreceptors (touch) and chemoreceptors (taste). They also have statocysts which help them to sense and correct their orientation, and light-sensitive cells that can detect a shadow (some have actual eyes, such as scallops, who have more complex eyes with a lens, a two-layered retina, and a concave mirror). Third, they do have a nervous system, which consists of a nerve network and a series of paired ganglia (they don't have a central nervous system but we know this doesn't matter if they still have enough interconnected neurons spread in different parts of the body). Fourth, research has found endogenous morphine (a natural analgesic) in specific bivalve tissues appears to be involved in the response to physical trauma. Fifth, they react to negative experiences appropriately.*
>
> *[…] Finally, we have the issue of mobility […] They do move, actually. Sometimes very slowly (as adult marine mussels can attach and detach byssal threads to attain a better position in the subtract), sometimes at mid-speed (as freshwater mussels have a muscular 'foot' that helps them burrow and move small distances), sometimes quite fast (as sea scallops swimming away from immediate danger), sometimes in their larva stages (as in marine mussels where the round microscopic larva drifts for three weeks to six months, before settling on a hard surface), sometimes they move parts of their bodies, which has the same effect of fleeing from a bad situation (such as closing their 'valves' to no longer be 'out there'), as in oysters and others.*

I know all the animal figurines and stuffed toys I own are not sentient, but casually greeting them reminds me I should ensure I don't deprive any sentient being I encounter of the respect they deserve, even if they look very different to me, or they hardly move. I also politely greet each aphid and caterpillar I meet on the plants of my small veganic garden when I carefully inspect them before I take the portion of my food share.

I always imagine they greet me back, and that makes me feel good.

Viewpoint 4

> *"Belief in human superiority is clearly deep-rooted."*

Humans Aren't As Unique as They Think They Are

Colin A. Chapman and Michael A. Huffman

In this viewpoint, two researchers explore why humans tend to put nonhuman animals and humans in separate categories of animal. Michael Huffman studies the evolution of social systems in primates and other animals. Colin Chapman's research focuses on the environment and social organization.

"Why Do We Want to Think Humans Are Special?," by Colin A. Chapman and Michael A. Huffman, *Animal Sentience*, July 6, 2018. Reprinted by permission.

As you read, consider the following questions:

1. Why do humans tend to put things in categories? Why can this sometimes be a problem?
2. Why, according to Chapman and Huffman, do we need to re-evaluate our notion of human uniqueness?
3. What decisions, according to these authors, might we make differently if we better understood and respected nonhuman life?

Humans have the propensity to place things into categories (i.e., good vs. bad, full vs. empty, black vs. white), which can directly shape how we view the world. Since categorization shapes our actions, it is important to evaluate their validity and distinctness and the degree to which one category blurs into the next. One categorization that has intrigued scholars for centuries is that of humans versus nonhuman animals. We often put humans on a pedestal, as unique and superior to all other animals: one of a kind; unlike any other animal. For example, in the 17th century, Rene Descartes stated that only people were creatures of reason, linked to the mind of God, while animals were merely machines made of flesh. His follower Nicolas Malebranche went on to say that animals "eat without pleasure, cry without pain, grow without knowing it: they desire nothing, fear nothing, know nothing." Today Descartes's and Malebranche's statements may seem extreme and wrong (Call, 2006), but they clearly reflect the propensity to see animals and humans as very different and humans as superior.

The view of humans and animals has changed since the 17th century (Fuentes, 2018; Marks, 2016; Van Schaik, 2016), thus these categories need to be reevaluated. Other categorizations have changed dramatically over time, with very positive effects on human societies. When the U.S. Declaration of Independence and Constitution were written, "only white male property holders [were] deemed adequately endowed to be included in the category of personhood" (US 1776). This is no longer the definition of personhood. In fact, the question of whether great apes warrant being accorded personhood is generating much academic interest today (Kurki and Pietrzykowski, 2017; Shyam, 2015; Wise, 2014).

A second reason to reevaluate the human/animal distinction is that many of our previous criteria for human uniqueness have proved wrong. Thomas Carlyle (1833) stated that "Man is a tool-using animal. Without tools he is nothing, with tools he is all" (Carlyle, 1833). This definition of "Man the Tool Maker" was largely viewed as true until the 1960s, when Jane Goodall's observations of chimpanzees (*Pan troglodytes*) using tools to extract termites from their mounds (with the help of publicity from *National Geographic*) eventually invalidated Carlyle's definition. It had taken well over a century (Goodall, 1986; Goodall, 1964). Prior to the Goodall findings, there had already been considerable evidence, largely ignored, that the definition was flawed. For example, in 1925 Köhler reported a series of simple experiments that clearly demonstrated chimpanzees could use tools and even cooperate in tool use to obtain food rewards. The chimpanzees would pile boxes one on top of another and then use sticks (even putting two sticks together) to reach a food reward hung high above their heads. Several primate species have now been shown to be habitual tool users, some maintaining tool-using cultures for hundreds of generations (Haslam et al., 2017).

Today we know that tools are also used by many non-primate species such as elephants (Hart and Hart, 1994), Caledonia crows (van Casteren, 2017), African grey parrots (Pepperberg, 2004), sea otters (Hall and Schaller, 1964; Fujii et al., 2014), rodents (Nagano and Aoyama, 2017), octopuses (Finn et al., 2009), and some fish (Bernardi, 2012). A similar failed criterion had been put forward in 1891 by Sir William Osler, who stated: "A desire to take medicine is, perhaps, the great feature which distinguishes man from other animals." The subsequent extensive documentation of medicinal plant use by chimpanzees and other primates opened the flood gates for research in this area (Huffman, 1997; Huffman, 2007), leading to examples of medicine use not only by other mammals (e.g., elephants, bears, civets, coatis, porcupines), but also birds (e.g., snow geese, finches, raptors) and insects (e.g., bumble bees, ants, butterflies) (Engel, 2002; Huffman, 2007).

Chu (2014) suggested that humans are unique in their ability to build complex structures. A number of authors have since echoed this (Fuentes, 2017; Marks, 2015) despite the evidence of complex living constructions by animals such as beavers (*Castor canadensis*), birds, bees and wasps (Doucet et al., 1994; Hansell, 2000; Hepburn et al., 2016). Termite mounds are remarkable structures with specific areas built for different purposes, elaborate features for draining water and cooling the mound, and even gardens to cultivate fungi as a source of food and medicine (Darlington, 1985; Korb, 2003; Korb, 2010).

These and many other such claims about putative defining differences between humans and animals span from 1833 to 2014 have proved wrong. Yet the desire to see humans as unique still remains. Is this a valid scientific question? One of the distinctive features of science is hypothesis testing (Cartmill, 1990; Popper, 1968). If hypotheses about human uniqueness repeatedly prove to be wrong for one trait after another, does this not imply that the hypothesis itself is wrong? We can keep resurrecting the hypothesis with new traits not yet considered, but to what end?

Evolutionary theory is a widely accepted explanation for the diversity of life on the planet. If uniqueness were intended to mean humans are one of a kind, unlike anything else, this would contradict evolution. Evolution consists of changes in genetically coded traits: if a new trait is advantageous for survival and reproduction in the environmental setting in which it occurs, its frequency will increase. Any trait (e.g., human intelligence) must have its roots in common ancestors; there are no "Hopeful

Monsters" as proposed by Goldschmidt (1940). Matt Cartmill (1990) summarized this well when reviewing some of the early critics of natural selection. Some scholars argued that natural selection could not account for some human traits, such as our intellectual capacities and our moral faculties, as they could not have been generated through survival of the fittest variants among ape-like ancestors. This argument was countered by Darwin (1871) and his followers who simply asserted that these traits had selective advantages and thus the moral and intellectual gap between humans and other higher mammals was only a matter of degree. All genetic traits are derived from predecessor traits; thus, there are similarities among the closest living relatives.

Many claims about the uniqueness of people state or imply that humans are superior to animals. In both Judaism and Christianity, humans are said to be made in the image of god and given dominion over lower creatures (Genesis). Aristotle believed that plants and animals were made for the sake of humans (Taylor, 1984). A number of religions in the Orient believe in the concept of a gradation of beings, with humans being the ultimate state. In Jainism there are four states with gods the highest, humans second, suffering in hell the third, and plants and animals last (Laidlaw, 1995). Belief in human superiority is clearly deep-rooted. When scholars make such assertions today, they often select traits on an ad hoc basis according to what they view as important among the things at which humans excel. Examples include the traits discussed above (tool use, medicine, construction). As part of Tetsuro Matsuzawa's 40 years of research on chimpanzee cognition (Matsuzawa, 2017), one candidate, the ability to solve complex problems, was examined in a beautiful study by Inoue and Matsuzawa (2007). They developed a memory test in which numbers were shown on a computer screen and then covered by opaque boxes. Chimpanzees were rewarded if they touched the boxes in the sequence that the numbers had been represented (i.e., 1 to 5). The researchers concluded that their study "shows that young chimpanzees can quickly grasp many numerals at a glance, with no decline in performance as the hold duration is varied. Moreover, the young ones showed better performance than adults in the memory task. Our study shows that young chimpanzees have an extraordinary working memory capability for numerical recollection, even better than that of human adults" (Inoue and Matsuzawa, 2007).

Claims of human superiority are used to justify human cruelty toward animals (Arluke, 2017), such as those raised for food (Taylor and Fraser, 2017). They mirror how claims of ethnic superiority are used to justify atrocities and even genocide against people trying to escape from famine or violence (Kunst et al., 2017; Staub, 1989).

We think it is time for our species to use our intellect to change our actions. This must start by recognizing that while differences exist between animals and humans or among cultures or peoples, they should not be ranked vertically. Differences are value-free and of interest because they provide diversity, whether genetic or cultural; studying them allows us to better understand ourselves. Problems arise only when a cultural belief infringes on the rights and safety of others (Mechoulan, 2017; Twining et al., 2000; Bauman et al., 2014).

There are many differences (and similarities) between human and nonhuman species, just as there are differences (and similarities) between any two species, any two cultures, or even any two individuals. However, since all traits cannot be taken into account simultaneously, it is inappropriate to accord superiority to a subset of traits that are preselected in a biased or ad-hoc fashion. Species can be compared on a suite of singled-out traits, as is done in multivariate university rankings, but the exercise is likely to be just as arbitrary.

We should use the traits we are so proud of — our vaunted intellect, communication skills, and morality — to create positive change. There is little doubt that now is the time when these skills are desperately needed. The world's ecosystems are in peril. Since our species is the major cause, we must provide solutions. Biodiversity is being lost at an accelerating rate, with current extinction rates approximately 1,000 times higher than background rates observed in the fossil record (Pimm et al., 2014). Extant vertebrate species have declined in abundance by approximately 25% since 1970 (Dirzo et al., 2014). Between 2000 and 2012, 2.3 million km2 of forest were lost globally, and in the tropics, tropical forest loss has increased annually (Hansen et al., 2013).

To put this in perspective, the area of forest lost is approximately the size of Mexico. Global estimates of the extent of wildlife over-exploitation are very poor; however, in Africa, four million metric tons of bushmeat are extracted each year from the Congo basin alone (equivalent to approximately 4,500,000 cows, or 80 million small (5 kg) monkeys). (Not all bushmeat is primate; Fa and Brown, 2009.) Global temperature is predicted to increase by 1.5°C by the end of the 21st century (IPCC, 2014) and researchers have projected that by 2100, 75% of all tropical forests present in 2000 will experience temperatures that are higher than the temperatures presently supporting closed canopy forests (Wright et al., 2009; Peres et al., 2016).

These statistics illustrate that we continue to place human profit ahead of the rights of animals and the ecosystems that support them, not to mention the rights of future human generations. An example of the drive for profit is that the conversion of forest to oil palm plantations was responsible for 3 million hectares of deforestation from 2000-2011 (an area the size of the Philippines) (Vijay et al., 2016). This was a significant factor leading to the loss of 100,000 orangutans between 1999 and 2015 (Voigt et al., 2018). Ever more land is projected to be needed for agricultural activities because of human population growth and people electing to eat higher up on the food chain (Delgado, 2003).

Yet this is also the time when people have options to use products not containing palm oil, to eat lower on the food chain, and to use products that do not support the deforestation of tropical forests. As the duration of inaction continues, the options available to society become progressively limited — climate change represents a clear example (IPCC, 2018).

Many human traits once thought unique to our species have proved to differ only in degree from those of many other species living on the planet. We cannot survive without many of those other species today; it is because of the existence of other species that we exist. We need to treat them with the respect they deserve and not judge their intelligence by how much they resemble us, nor evaluate them only on the basis of what they provide us. We need to acknowledge how much we resemble them and how much we have to learn from them. Doing so will allow us to make decisions—such as whether to use palm oil or how high on the food chain to eat—with a realistic understanding of the consequences of our actions, for them as well as for us.

References

Arluke, A. (2017) *Just a dog: Understanding animal cruelty and ourselves*. Temple University Press.

Bauman, Z., Bigo, D., Esteves, P., Guild, E., Jabri, V., Lyon, D. & Walker, R. B. (2014) After Snowden: Rethinking the impact of surveillance. *International Political Sociology*, 8, 121-144.

Bernardi, G. (2012) The use of tools by wrasses (Labridae). *Coral Reefs*, 31, 39.

Call, J. (2006) Descartes' two errors: Reason and reflection in the great apes. In *Rational animals?* (S. Hurley & M. Nudds, Eds.). Oxford: Oxford University Press.

Carlyle, T. (1833) Sartor resartus (meaning 'the tailor re-tailored'). *Fraser's Magazine*.

Cartmill, M. (1990) Human uniqueness and theoretical content in paleoanthropology. *International Journal of Primatology*, 11, 173-192.

Darlington, J. P. (1985) The structure of mature mounds of the termite *Macrotermes michaelseni* in Kenya. *International Journal of Tropical Insect Science*, 6, 149-156.

Delgado, C. L. (2003) Rising consumption of meat and milk in developing countries has created a new food revolution. *The Journal of Nutrition*, 133, 3907S-3910S.

Dirzo, R., Young, H. S., Galetti, M., Ceballos, G., Isaac, N. J. B. & Collen, B. (2014) Defaunation in the Anthropocene. *Science*, 345, 401-406.

Doucet, C. M., Adams, I. T. & Fryxell, J. M. (1994) Beaver dam and cache composition: Are woody species used differently? *Ecoscience*, 1, 268-270.

Engel, C. (2002) *Wild health*. Boston: Houghton Mifflin.

Fa, J. E. & Brown, D. (2009) Impacts of hunting on mammals in African tropical moist forests: A review and synthesis. *Mammal Review*, 39, 231-264.

Finn, J. K., Tregenza, T. & Norman, M. D. (2009) Defensive tool use in a coconut-carrying octopus. *Current Biology*, 19, R1069-R1070.

Fuentes, A. (2017) Human niche, human behaviour, human nature. *Interface Focus*, 7, 20160136.

Fuentes, A. (2018) How humans and apes are different, and why it matters. *Journal of Anthropological Research*, 74, 151-167.
Fujii, J. A., Ralls, K. & Tinker, M. T. (2014) Ecological drivers of variation in tool-use frequency across sea otter populations. *Behavioral Ecology*, 26, 519-526.
Goldschmidt, R. (1940) The material basis of evolution. New Haven: Yale University Press.
Goodall, J. (1964) Tool-using and aimed throwing in a community of free-living chimpanzees. *Nature*, 201, 1264.
Goodall, J. (1986) *The chimpanzees of Gombe: Patterns of behaviour*. London: Harvard University Press.
Hall, K. & Schaller, G. B. (1964) Tool-using behavior of the California sea otter. *Journal of Mammalogy*, 45, 287-298.
Hansell, M. (2000) *Bird nests and construction behaviour*. Cambridge University Press.
Hansen, M. C., Potapov, P. V., Moore, R., Hancher, M., Turubanova, S. A., Tyukavina, A., Thau, D., Stehman, S. V., Goetz, S. J., Loveland, T. R., Kommareddy, A., Egorov, A., Chini, L., Justice, C. O. & Townshend, J. R. G. (2013) High-resolution global maps of 21st-century forest cover change. *Science*, 342, 850-853.
Hart, B. L. & Hart, L. A. (1994) Fly switching by Asian elephants: Tool use to control parasites. *Animal Behaviour*, 48, 35-45.
Haslam, M., Hernandez-Aguilar, R. A., Proffitt, T., Arroyo, A., Falótico, T., Fragaszy, D., Gumert, M., Harris, J. W., Huffman, M. A. & Kalan, A. K. (2017) Primate archaeology evolves. *Nature Ecology & Evolution*, 1, 1431.
Hepburn, H., Pirk, C. & Duangphakdee, O. (2016) *Honeybee nests*. Springer.
Huffman, M. A. (1997) Current evidence for self-medication in primates: A multidisciplinary perspective. *Yearbook of Physical Anthropology*, 40, 171-200.
Huffman, M. A. (2007) Primate self-medication. In *Primates in perspective* (C. J. Campbell, A. Fuentes, K. C. MacKinnon, M. Panger & S. K. Bearder, Eds.), pp. 677-690. Oxford: Oxford University Press.
Huffman, M. A., Gotoh, S., Turner, L. A., Hamai, M. & Yoshida, K. (1997) Seasonal trends in intestinal nematode infection and medicinal plant use among chimpanzees in the Mahale Mountains, Tanzania. *Primates*, 38, 111-125.
Inoue, S. & Matsuzawa, T. (2007) Working memory of numerals in chimpanzees. *Current Biology*, 17, R1004-R1005.
IPCC (2014) *Climate change 2014: Synthesis report. Contribution of working groups I, II and III to the fifth assessment report of the Intergovernmental Panel on Climate Change* (Core Writing Team, R. K. Pachauri and L. A. Meyer, Eds.). Geneva, Switzerland: IPPC.
IPCC (2018) *Global warming of 1.5°C*. Geneva, Switzerland: IPCC.
Köhler, W. (1925) T*he mentality of apes* (translated from the second revised edition by E. Winter). London: Kegan Paul, Trench, Trubner.
Korb, J. (2003) Thermoregulation and ventilation of termite mounds. *Naturwissenschaften*, 90, 212-219.
Korb, J. (2010) Termite mound architecture, from function to construction. *Biology of termites: A modern synthesis*, pp. 349-373. Springer.
Kunst, J. R., Fischer, R., Sidanius, J. & Thomsen, L. (2017) Preferences for group dominance track and mediate the effects of macro-level social inequality and violence across societies. *Proceedings of the National Academy of Sciences*, 201616572.
Kurki, V. A. & Pietrzykowski, T. (2017) *Legal personhood: Animals, artificial intelligence and the unborn*. Springer

Laidlaw, J. (1995) *Riches and renunciation: Religion, economy, and society among the Jains.* Oxford University Press.

Marks, J. (2015) *Tales of the ex-apes: How we think about human evolution.* University of California Press.

Marks, J. (2016) Tales of the ex-apes. *General Anthropology*, 23, 1-7.

Matsuzawa, T. (2017) The 40th anniversary of the Ai Project: The commemorative gift is a silk scarf painted by Ai the chimpanzee. *Primates*, 58, 261-265.

Mechoulan, S. (2017, winter) The European case against the face-veil. *International Journal of Constitutional Law.*

Nagano, A. & Aoyama, K. (2017) Tool-use by rats (*Rattus norvegicus*): Tool-choice based on tool features. *Animal Cognition*, 20, 199-213.

Osler, W. (1891) Recent Advances in Medicine. Science 17: 170–171

Pepperberg, I. M. (2004) "Insightful" string-pulling in Grey parrots (*Psittacus erithacus*) is affected by vocal competence. *Animal Cognition*, 7, 263-266.

Peres, C. A., Emilio, T., Schietti, J., Desmoulière, S. J. & Levi, T. (2016) Dispersal limitation induces long-term biomass collapse in overhunted Amazonian forests. *Proceedings of the National Academy of Sciences*, 113, 892-897.

Pimm, S. L., Jenkins, C. N., Abell, R., Brooks, T. M., Gittleman, J. L., Joppa, L. N., Raven, P. H., Roberts, C. M. & Sexton, J. O. (2014) The biodiversity of species and their rates of extinction, distribution, and protection. *Science*, 344, 1246752.

Popper, K. R. (1968) *Conjectures and refutations: The growth of scientific knowledge.* New York: Harper & Row.

Shyam, G. (2015) The legal status of animals: The world rethinks its position. *Alternative Law Journal*, 40, 266-270.

Staub, E. (1989) *The roots of evil: The origins of genocide and other group violence.* Cambridge, UK: Cambridge University Press.

Taylor, N. & Fraser, H. (2017) Slaughterhouses: The language of life, the discourse of death. In *The palgrave international handbook of animal abuse studies*, pp. 179-199. Springer.

Taylor, P. W. (1984) Are humans superior to plants and animals? *Environmental Ethics*, 6, 149-160.

Twining, H., Arluke, A. & Patronek, G. (2000) Managing the stigma of outlaw breeds: A case study of pit bull owners. *Society & Animals*, 8, 25-52.

van Casteren, A. (2017) Tool use: Crows craft the right tool for the job. *Current Biology*, 27, R1314-R1316.

Van Schaik, C. P. (2016) *The primate origins of human nature.* New York: John Wiley & Sons, Inc.

Vijay, V., Pimm, S. L., Jenkins, C. N. & Smith, S. J. (2016) The impacts of oil palm on recent deforestation and biodiversity loss. *PLoS ONE*, 11, e0159668.

Voigt, M., Wich, S. A., Ancrenaz, M., Meijaard, E., Abram, N., Banes, G. L., Campbell-Smith, G., d'Arcy, L. J., Delgado, R. A. & Erman, A. (2018) Global demand for natural resources eliminated more than 100,000 Bornean orangutans. *Current Biology*, 28, 761-769, e5.

Wise, S. (2014) *Rattling the cage: Toward legal rights for animals.* Da Capo Press. Wright, S. J., Muller-Landau, H. C. & Schipper, J. (2009) The future of tropical species on a warmer planet. *Conservation Biology*, 23, 1418-1426.

VIEWPOINT 5

"Freedom is fundamental to welfare."

Some Animals Should Never Be Kept as Pets

Dr. Emma Milne

So far in this volume, the viewpoints have focused on wild animals and farm animals. Now, the focus is put on pets and the ethics of pet ownership. Here, the author argues that some animals should never be kept as pets. Emma Milne is a veterinarian and former trustee of the Animal Welfare Foundation. She lives in France.

"Exotic Pets—Ethical or Not?," by Dr. Emma Milne, Freedom for Animals, October 5, 2022. Reprinted by permission.

As you read, consider the following questions:

1. What are the five basic welfare needs, as described here?
2. What are some of the practical and ethical challenges of feeding pets, according to Milne?
3. Why is it virtually impossible to provide the proper environment for some animals?

I qualified as a vet in 1996 and back then, Chinchillas were about the most exotic pet we might come across. In the couple of decades since then, the popularity of all manner of exotic pets has rocketed, from geckos to snakes to spiders. In fact, one time when I was being filmed for *Vets in Practice* a client told me they were going to bring in their red-backed spider the following week because it was losing its hair. I had not a clue about these creatures so did some research and found out that the major cause of hair loss in these spiders was the stress of being handled. It gave me the perfect excuse not to handle it!

But this brings up an important point: How many wild animals that we keep in captivity are chronically stressed by the whole experience? When we take a non-native species and try to keep it somewhere fundamentally different can we ever really recreate the habitat that they would prefer? All too often the answer is no, and this is why many exotic pets are presented to vets with diseases related to their nutrition and environment.

Whenever I think about animal keeping and welfare I love to do it from the point of view of the five basic welfare needs. And we need to remember that these really are the most basic things. So let's go through them and see if we can really reconcile the keeping of exotic pets.

The Need for the Right Food and Fresh Water

This seems pretty obvious but you would be amazed how difficult it can be to get right, even for the mainstream pets like dogs, cats and rabbits. Exotic wild animals have vastly varied diets depending on the species and where they originate. Their anatomy and physiology is often starkly different from mammals. Some of the reptiles may only need feeding very infrequently and this can be difficult for owners to accept. Humans love to feed animals, it's a big part of the human-animal bond and also a reason that the majority of pets now are overweight.

Many of these animals catch and eat live prey and even if we provide inanimate substitutes, some animals will not recognise it as food. It needs to be warm and moving to trigger the desire to eat. This presents another ethical dilemma; how do we care for the welfare of the animals being eaten as well as the pet who needs to eat?

The need for the Right Environment

I think, for me this is one of the biggest reasons I am against the keeping of exotic pets. For many of these species we are simply failing to provide anything like the right environment. Some originate in very sunny, hot, arid environments and we take them to northern Europe and try to recreate a mini desert in a glass tank.

Many of the animals rely heavily on ultraviolet light, as well as a good diet, for production of minerals like calcium. In practice vets see reptiles all the time with metabolic bone diseases and pathological fractures because they simply aren't getting enough light.

Too often the enclosures are too small to allow for an area that has a UV light and enough room for a shaded section. Add to this the need for pools of water for some of the species to swim or bathe in and you can see that many set-ups will be woefully inadequate.

I think it's particularly depressing when people have a vivarium and put a picture of a rocky desert at the back of it as if this is going to make the poor creature feel more at home! Like giving a prisoner a mural of a beautiful beach restaurant and thinking that will help the monotony and frustration of life in a cell.

I'd also like to seriously question this assumption that snakes do not need an enclosure large enough for them to stretch out fully. Who made this rule? What on earth makes us think that we should accept, as good welfare, that *any* animal can never fully extend its body if it wants to? Humans too often neglect the needs of the animals they keep because the needs are inconvenient. This is unacceptable. If we can't meet these needs or don't want to, then the choice of pet is wrong.

The Need to Be Protected from Pain, Injury and Disease

I'm sure you will have guessed by now that we are failing here because of what I've said before. Too many exotic pets have the wrong nutrition and potentially dangerous environments.

We also have the problem that we don't yet understand all there is to know about diseases and for general practitioner vets this can be very difficult. Even from the medication point of view, most drugs are developed for mammals so safety data in other species can be lacking.

The Need to Be With or Without Other Animals and the Need to Behave Normally

I've lumped these two together because they are inextricably linked. I view these as the needs for mental, rather than physical, wellbeing. These are so vitally important. We *must* consider these to be as important as the other three, if not more. Animals should be happy as well as healthy.

My husband is a vet too and he did a lot more exotic work in practice than I did. He would often see bearded dragons with lesions on their noses where they had run repeatedly into the sides of the tank, trying to escape. I find this incredibly sad.

I do a lot of welfare and ethics and many of our mainstream pets' behaviour is misunderstood. We keep cats with other cats when they find it stressful and we keep rabbits on their own when they absolutely need rabbit company because they are social animals. How can we possibly hope to understand the behavioural needs of hundreds of other species? *And* then get them right?

I live in the south of France and we are lucky to see geckos every day. When you see how much they explore to hunt and see them basking in the beautiful sunshine it's impossible to imagine that we can ever replicate that life in a tank. If you see an iguana swim across a whole lake and climb a tree, how can we ever reconcile keeping one in an enclosure that is barely longer than the creature itself?

I think we still don't look after our 'normal' pets well enough. I also think that wild animals belong in the wild. Life in captivity is miserable for most animals, in my opinion.

I would even go as far to say that *any* animal that needs to be in a cage or a tank shouldn't be kept as a pet. We will never meet the needs of these animals fully because they are not free. And freedom is fundamental to welfare.

> *"Individually, no criterion can prove an animal is sentient. None is a smoking gun. But, the more criteria an animal meets, the more likely sentience becomes."*

We Need to Consider the Possibility of Sentience in Invertebrates

Andrew Crump

In the closing viewpoint in this chapter, the author comes back to the basic question of sentience and how we define it. Andrew Crump is a lecturer in animal cognition and welfare at the Royal Veterinary College and a postdoctoral biologist in ASENT, a project that aims to find ways to resolve debates about animal sentience.

"Invertebrate Sentience, Welfare, & Policy" by Andrew Crump, partially sourced by Gibbons, M., Crump, A., & Chittka, L. (2022) and Schnell, A., Crump, A., & Birch, J. (2021), London School of Economics and Political Science. Reprinted by Permission.

As you read, consider the following questions:

1. Why, according to Crump, is animal sentience so difficult to study scientifically?
2. What criteria did Crump and colleagues use to study the possibility of sentience in cephalopod molluscs and decapod crustaceans?
3. What evidence did they find for sentience in insects?

The Significance of Sentience

Imagine two entities: a pebble and a poodle. Now imagine I leave both in the back of a hot car. Presumably you'd worry about the welfare of one of these entities (the poodle) and not the other (the pebble), even if the hot car damaged both. But why? In other words, when we talk about *animal* welfare, why restrict our moral concern to animals? Why not plants, bacteria, or pebbles?

The answer, I think, is that we generally consider animals to be *sentient*. Sentience is the capacity to have feelings: positive or negative mental states like pain, pleasure, anger, excitement, and fear. The poodle is almost certainly sentient, whereas the pebble almost certainly isn't. Leaving the poodle in a hot car *feels bad* from the poodle's perspective. The poodle can experience pain and suffering; the pebble cannot.

This raises another question: are *all* animals sentient? Animal welfare ethics, science, and policy overwhelmingly focus on vertebrate animals. For example, primates in labs; cows, pigs, and chickens on farms; and dogs and cats in our homes. There is a broad scientific consensus that these mammals and birds are sentient, and that we should at least consider their welfare.

But 95% of animal species are *invertebrates*, including groups like the cephalopod molluscs (octopus, squid, and cuttlefish), decapod crustaceans (crabs, lobsters, and shrimp), and insects. These unnoticed, hyper-numerous animals face substantial welfare issues. Octopuses may be asphyxiated or beaten to death;

lobsters can be boiled alive; and beetles are slowly dissolved using pesticides[1]. Do invertebrates suffer as a result, or are these harms equivalent to leaving a pebble in a hot car?

This isn't just an academic question. When drafting animal welfare law, legislators must decide which animals to protect. The UK's Animal Welfare (Sentience) Act 2022, for example, originally defined "animal" as any vertebrate besides humans. This would have meant that no invertebrates were recognised as sentient.

On the LSE's Foundations of Animal Sentience Project, we're tackling big questions like which animals are sentient, and how should we treat sentient animals? Here, I'll summarise the evidence for sentience in cephalopods, decapods, and insects, and discuss the legal implications for their welfare.

Why Is Sentience Difficult to Study?

The question of invertebrate sentience is tough to answer. Feelings like pain are inherently private experiences. Moreover, pain can be distinguished from *nociception*: the processing of harmful stimuli, which may lead to reflexive responses. Scientists have long known that invertebrates display nociception. However, if an animal detects and responds to potentially damaging stimuli, it is not necessarily an indicator of pain.. However, if an animal detects and responds to potentially damaging stimuli, it is not necessarily an indicator of pain.

Nociception and pain can happen, to some extent, independently of each other. If you touch a hot stove, for instance, you'll pull your hand away and feel a painful burn. But you pull your hand away *before* you feel the burn. Nerve signals from your hand travel to the spinal cord, where they take two separate pathways[2]. The first pathway is back to the arm muscles, causing you to withdraw your hand. The second pathway is to the brain, where pain is felt. So hand withdrawal is a nociceptive reflex, which doesn't require pain.

This difficulty of diagnosing pain in non-verbal beings is illustrated by the relatively recent treatment of babies during surgery. Into the 1980s, many surgeons believed babies could not feel pain and rarely used anaesthetics. They thought babies' obvious responses, such as screaming and writhing, were "just reflexes"[3]. Even though we still can't prove babies feel pain, most now accept they do with near certainty.

For any being that cannot talk about its feelings, we need to rely on common sense and probability. The more sentience indicators found, the higher the probability of sentience. It's important to use consistent criteria across animals, and to look for similar sentience indicators across invertebrates and vertebrates.

How to Evaluate Evidence for Sentience

In 2020, the UK government asked my colleagues and I to assess the evidence for sentience in cephalopod molluscs and decapod crustaceans. They wanted to know whether animal welfare legislation should cover these invertebrates.

How can we find out if an animal is sentient? It's tempting to think we only need to look at whether they try to avoid or escape being injured. However, as discussed above, other animals might only respond reflexively to injury, without experiencing pain.

For our investigation, we used eight scientific criteria for determining sentience. The first four addressed whether the animal's nervous system could support sentience. We wanted to find out whether it could detect harmful stimuli and transmit those signals to the brain. And, also, whether the signals were processed in integrative brain regions: parts of the brain that bring together information from many sources. Finally, it was important to understand whether anaesthetics or painkillers changed the nervous system response.

Our four remaining criteria focused on the animal's behaviour. Could it trade off risks of injury against opportunities for a reward? Did individuals tend to the specific site of an injury, and could they learn to avoid stimuli associated with injury? We also investigated whether they valued anaesthetics or painkillers when injured. These behaviours distinguish rigid and reflexive reactions to injury, such as withdrawing a burnt hand, from flexible responses, so they are taken as evidence of pain.

Individually, no criterion can prove an animal is sentient. None is a smoking gun. But, the more criteria an animal meets, the more likely sentience becomes.

Using this framework, we produced a comprehensive report on cephalopod and decapod sentience, which reviewed over 300 scientific studies[4][5][6]. We followed this up with a paper evaluating the evidence for sentience in insects[7]. The results were startling.

Evidence for Sentience in Invertebrates

We found the strongest evidence for sentience in cephalopods. Octopuses were the stars. With around 170 million brain cells, they have higher brain-to-body ratios than most reptiles and fish. This allows octopuses to perform remarkable feats of learning and memory.

Octopuses also behave in ways that point to experiences of pain. For example, in a recent study, they were given three chambers to explore[8]. Injection with acetic acid in their initially preferred chamber led to octopuses subsequently avoiding that chamber. Injured octopuses learnt to prefer an alternative chamber, where local anaesthetic was available. This anaesthetic silenced nerve activity between the injury site and the brain. Similar findings in mammals are said to indicate pain.

Decapods also displayed compelling signs of sentience. For instance, one high-profile study allowed crayfish to explore a cross-shaped tank[9]. Two arms of the cross were illuminated, whereas the other two were shaded. In the wild, crayfish use dark shelters to hide from predators, so time spent in the shaded arms was taken to measure anxiety-like behaviour. Exposure to an electric field caused crayfish to avoid the light arms. Administering an anti-anxiety drug reversed the effect[10]. These findings reveal that crayfish have mental states with similar brain mechanisms and behaviour to anxiety.

There is also striking evidence for sentience in insects. In a recent study led by PhD student Matilda Gibbons, we discovered that bumblebee responses to heat depend on other motivations[11]. We gave bumblebees four feeders: two heated and two unheated. Each feeder dispensed sugar water, which bumblebees love. When every feeder contained the same concentration of sugar water, bees avoided the two heated feeders. But, when the heated feeders dispensed sweeter sugar water than the unheated feeders, bumblebees often chose the heated feeders. Their love of sugar outweighed their hatred of heat. This suggests bees feel pain, because (like humans) their responses were more than just reflexes. Bees also remembered the heated and unheated feeders, and they used this memory to decide which to feed from. So, the trade-off happened in the brain—where pain is generated in humans.

How Should We Interpret the Evidence?

Despite striking evidence for sentience in a handful of well-studied invertebrates, there are 750 cephalopod species, 15,000 decapod species, and a whopping one million insect species. By way of comparison, there are only around 4,000 mammal species. Invertebrates' staggering diversity means that sentience has never been studied in most species.

Take insects. Flies and cockroaches satisfy six of our criteria, which amounts to "strong evidence" for pain (according to this framework). Beetles, meanwhile, only satisfy two criteria. But, like other insects that received low scores, there are very few studies on beetles in this context. So absence of evidence is not evidence of absence. Indeed, we've found no convincing evidence of any insect, cephalopod, or decapod failing a criterion.

This is not just an invertebrate issue—sentience has never been studied in most vertebrate species either. With vertebrates, we routinely generalise from laboratory species (such as rats and zebrafish) to related species. Invertebrates should be treated in the same way. That means protecting under-studied animals if it's reasonable to generalise from strong evidence in a better-studied species.

Using this reasoning, our report recommended treating all cephalopods and decapods as sentient. The UK government responded by amending the Animal Welfare (Sentience) Bill (now Act, 2022) to cover both groups of invertebrates. Cephalopods and decapods are now legally recognised as sentient, and lawmakers must pay "due regard" to their welfare.

Unfinished Business

Recognising sentience in cephalopods and decapods was a milestone, but there is much left to do. Most of the UK's other animal welfare laws still don't cover these animals. As such, whilst decapods and cephalopods have a legally recognised capacity to suffer, there is essentially no legal force to prevent someone causing them extreme and unnecessary pain.

To regulate specific practices, the government would need to extend the Animal Welfare Act 2006, which only covers vertebrates. This law makes it an offence to cause "unnecessary suffering" to protected animals. Expanding its scope to include certain invertebrates could mean that shellfish aquaculture, like conventional farms, would need to minimise animal suffering and use humane slaughter methods.

The Animals (Scientific Procedures) Act 1986 regulates the use of protected animals in science. Covering decapods under this act, as cephalopods already are, could reduce the number tested and ensure that experiments have a strong scientific rationale.

My colleagues and I are talking to the government about these issues. We've met with MPs in parliament and hosted a workshop at the LSE, where Home Office representatives, NGOs, and scientists discussed regulating decapod research. There's a broad cross-party consensus that the inconsistent coverage between animal welfare laws is unsustainable. Hopefully, that will soon change.

And then there's insects. According to our framework, the evidence for sentience in at least some insects is equivalent to the evidence for sentience in cephalopods and decapods. Yet insects are not covered under the Animal Welfare (Sentience) Act 2022 or any other UK welfare legislation.

I think animal welfare law should protect insects. Our recent paper encouraged insect researchers to think about welfare during their experiments[12]. And I recently spoke at Defra's internal seminar series, championing insects and their inclusion in the Animal Welfare (Sentience) Act 2022.

I hope our work has started a wider conversation about how to treat invertebrates humanely, so we can minimise their pain and suffering. Industry already considers many methods, such as electrical stunning and rapid slaughter, to be best practice. Promoting and enforcing these could protect producers against the erosion of standards, and reassure consumers that invertebrates receive high welfare standards.

This post borrows from two articles:

Gibbons, M., Crump, A., & Chittka, L. (2022). Insects may feel pain, says growing evidence—here's what this means for animal welfare laws. *The Conversation.*

Schnell, A., Crump, A., & Birch, J. (2021). Octopus, crabs and lobsters feel pain—this is how we found out. *The Conversation.*

Notes

[1] Crump, A., Browning, H., Schnell, A. K., Burn, C., & Birch, J. (2022). Invertebrate sentience and sustainable seafood. *Nature Food, 3*(11), 884-886.

[2] Defrin, R., Peleg, S., Weingarden, H., Heruti, R., & Urca, G. (2007). Differential effect of supraspinal modulation on the nociceptive withdrawal reflex and pain sensation. *Clinical Neurophysiology, 118*(2), 427-437.

[3] De Lima, J., Lloyd-Thomas, A. R., Howard, R. F., Sumner, E., & Quinn, T. M. (1996). Infant and neonatal pain: anaesthetists' perceptions and prescribing patterns. *British Medical Journal, 313*(7060), 787.

[4] Birch, J., Burn, C., Schnell, A., Browning, H., & Crump, A. (2021). *Review of the evidence of sentience in cephalopod molluscs and decapod crustaceans.* Defra.

[5] Crump, A., Browning, H., Schnell, A., Burn, C., & Birch, J. (2022). Sentience in decapod crustaceans: A general framework and review of the evidence. *Animal Sentience, 7*(32), 1.

[6] Crump, A., Browning, H., Schnell, A. K., Burn, C., & Birch, J. (2022). Animal sentience research: Synthesis and proposals. *Animal Sentience, 7.*

[7] Gibbons, M., Crump, A., Barrett, M., Sarlak, S., Birch, J., & Chittka, L. (2022). Can insects feel pain? A review of the neural and behavioural evidence. *Advances in Insect Physiology, 63*, 155-229.

[8] Crook, R. J. (2021). Behavioral and neurophysiological evidence suggests affective pain experience in octopus. *Iscience, 24*(3).

[9] Fossat, P., Bacqué-Cazenave, J., De Deurwaerdère, P., Delbecque, J. P., & Cattaert, D. (2014). Anxiety-like behavior in crayfish is controlled by serotonin. *Science, 344*(6189), 1293-1297.

[10] Fossat, P., Bacqué-Cazenave, J., De Deurwaerdère, P., Cattaert, D., & Delbecque, J. P. (2015). Serotonin, but not dopamine, controls the stress response and anxiety-like behavior in the crayfish Procambarus clarkii. *Journal of experimental biology, 218*(17), 2745-2752.

[11] Gibbons, M., Versace, E., Crump, A., Baran, B., & Chittka, L. (2022). Motivational trade-offs and modulation of nociception in bumblebees. *Proceedings of the National Academy of Sciences, 119*(31), e2205821119.

[12] Crump, A., Gibbons, M., Barrett, M., Birch, J., & Chittka, L. (2023). Is it time for insect researchers to consider their subjects' welfare?. *PLoS Biology, 21*(6), e3002138.

Periodical and Internet Sources Bibliography

The following articles have been selected to supplement the diverse views presented in this chapter.

Dane Charbeneau, “How Animal Equality in India is Creating Change for Animals,” Animal Equality, November 29. 2021, updated July 21, 2022. https://animalequality.org/blog/india-giant-steps-forward/.

Nicola Clayton and Alexandra Schnell, “Why invertebrates should be included in animal welfare protections,” *New Scientist*, 28 July 2021. https://www.newscientist.com/article/mg25133452-200-why-invertebrates-should-be-included-in-animal-welfare-protections/.

Benjamin K. Diggles, et al, “Reasons to Be Skeptical about Sentience and Pain in Fishes and Aquatic Invertebrates,” *Reviews in Fisheries Science & Aquaculture*, 4 October 2023. https://www.tandfonline.com/doi/full/10.1080/23308249.2023.2257802#abstract.

Ali Francis, “Do Fish Feel Pain?” *Bon Appétit*, March 15, 2023. https://www.bonappetit.com/story/do-fish-feel-pain?srsltid=AfmBOorRQEbqz2NXWyuY1Knxeh3QKKHK_-Ngi6H0ax4jlIgg8K2dV98w.

Vicki Hird, “Do worms feel pain and are ants happy? Why the science on invertebrate feelings is evolving,” *The Guardian*, 25 February 2025. https://www.theguardian.com/environment/2025/feb/25/do-worms-feel-pain-are-ants-happy-science-of-invertebrate-feelings.

Jasna Hodžić, “The inner life of a lobster: Do invertebrates have emotions?” *Big Think*, April 25, 2022. https://bigthink.com/life/do-invertebrates-have-emotions/.

Avery Elizabeth Hurt, “Invertebrates Are Pretty Clever, but Are They Conscious?” *Science News Explores*, November 16, 2023. https://www.snexplores.org/article/are-invertebrates-conscious-spiders-bees-crabs.

Ferris Jabr, “Fish Feel Pain. Now What?” *Hakai*, January 2, 2018. https://hakaimagazine.com/features/fish-feel-pain-now-what/.

Seth Millstein, “Lobsters Feel Pain When Boiled Alive, and Here’s How Science Knows,” *Sentience Science*, December 20, 2023. https://sentientmedia.org/do-lobsters-feel-pain/.

Helen Proctor, "Animal Sentience: Where are We and Where are We Heading?" *Animals*, 14 November 2012. https://www.mdpi.com/2076-2615/2/4/628.

Kevin Schneider. "The Case of Laxmi the Elephant and Animal Rights in India," Nonhuman Rights Project, August 14, 2020. https://www.nonhumanrights.org/blog/laxmi-animal-rights-india/.

OPPOSING VIEWPOINTS® SERIES

Chapter 4

What Would Be the Consequences if We Afforded Rights to Nonhuman Animals?

Chapter Preface

There is a lot to consider when discussing whether or not to grant rights for nonhuman animals. One of those things is the potential consequences of granting those rights. Authors in previous chapters have raised the possibility of a world in which a person could be arrested for stepping on a roach. If insects have rights, how do we protect ourselves from the diseases some carry? How do we grow food for ourselves without harming the insects that feed on those crops? These and other questions are extremely difficult to address.

One of the reasons often cited for protecting animals is to protect the environment and ecosystems we all depend on to survive. That's why many people eat less meat or have given it up altogether. However, that's a complicated equation. In the first viewpoint in this chapter, the author argues that restoring healthy ecosystems requires responsible land management.

Another viewpoint argues for protecting the oceans as a way of protecting the rights of all animals, including humans. One author gets imaginative: What would the world look like if animals had rights?

A pair of researchers from Australia point out that medical science—one area where using animals seem unavoidable—is already moving toward non-animal models. But first, let's look at how animals affect the ecosystem.

Viewpoint 1

"[B]eef raised in its environs beats a bean field any day as an ecologically just source of protein."

'Eat Less Meat' Ignores the Role of Animals in the Ecosystem

Ariel Greenwood

Animal rights necessarily involve the ecosystems animals live in as well as the animals themselves. In this essay, the author argues that protecting the environment means not giving up meat, but eating the right meat. Ariel Greenwood is a grazing manager for Freestone Ranch, a restoration-focused grass-fed beef operation in the northern San Francisco Bay Area, and works for Fibershed and the Occidental Arts and Ecology Center.

"'Eat Less Meat' Ignores the Role of Animals in the Ecosystem," by Ariel Greenwood, Civil Eats, January 26, 2018. Reprinted by permission.

As you read, consider the following questions:

1. Why does simply eating less meat not help the environment, according to Greenwood?
2. How does this author describe her work as a grazing manager?
3. How does eating meat from farms like the one Greenwood manages help other animals, such as owls, foxes, and bears?

Given the concerns over resource-intensive industrial meat production, you'd think the resounding message would be, "don't buy cheap meat, buy good meat."

Instead, a rule of thumb that has emerged in environmentalists' circles is simply "eat less meat." This statement frames meat as an indulgence rather than 1) the end result of an essential and timeless ecological process (the biological breakdown of vegetation, which feeds the soil and removes dead grass so that new vegetation can grow) and 2) a fulcrum in the way land across the world is managed or mismanaged.

As a grazier and land manager, I'm part of a growing group of people who have committed our lives to restoring the health of environments directly, through exquisitely precise grazing on sensitive land, and who depend on the support of our communities to do this work.

"Eat less meat" is a well-intended caveat amongst woke environmentalists (a group who is, after all, my cohort) but it has also become a primary barrier to me and others like me doing our work. And it's hard to not take that personally. Because what could be more personal than the health of my watershed and the kingdoms that inhabit it? If these things aren't personal to you, we have a bigger problem.

Our work goes like this: We memorize every nook and cranny of a piece of land like a lover's body. We study how water flows across it and what grasses grow where. We plant trees where we've seen them grow before and could grow again. We spend unpaid hours moving animals exactly where they need to go to knock down encroaching brush on long-neglected land. We fence out bird nests. We leave areas ungrazed for a season—and can calculate the cost to the tune of hundreds of dollars—because we know in our throats, our chests, our bellies, and our bones (that's where we feel it) that it needs another season to grow before grazing would be helpful. We get knocked down, kicked, cut up and cut open; we don't just risk injury but accept its inevitability. We memorize the names of species that used to grow or live here but have been lost. We love the land and its inhabitants so much that we're willing to work for next to nothing.

But martyrdom isn't very becoming, and you can't milk a dry cow; so like everyone else, graziers have to make money. Until environmentalists actually really put their money where their mouth is and pay me and others to graze land right without meat as the chief goal, we have to sell the surplus from our herds (the flesh of some of the animals) in order to be able to afford to feed ourselves.

Believe me, I wish I were a photosynthesizing autotroph who could get my nourishment directly from the sun.

Not all grazing is created equal. This is the essence of what gets missed in discussions about the impact of livestock agriculture on our local ecosystems and global climate. Decades of mismanagement has left a tough legacy for those of us grazing with restorative goals to overcome. But when animals are managed according to nature's schedule, beautiful changes can happen fast.

Some of the year I graze the animals in tight bunches to lay down old grass to feed the soil. Other times, I'm herding them fast across the property to stimulate grass plants to grow denser and healthier while they pump carbon deep into the soil food web. I can stop erosion around streams based on how I move these big animals, and stabilize vulnerable hillsides through careful decision-making. For me and many like me, grazing is our art form it's our best tool for breathing new life into neglected land.

"Eat less meat" is about mitigating damage, and it misses the opportunity to tell people that there's a way to actually benefit their planet. Industrially produced meat is unquestionably bad for the environment, and for animals. But perpetuating the myth that all meat is the same means that the potential benefits of responsibly raised meat never get a sufficient foothold. By telling only half the story, we're perpetuating the problem because we never bother to mention the solution.

As an aside, few environmentalists who are opposed to grazing animals and eating their flesh have demonstrated either the degree of embodied affection, personal risk, and deep practice or the knowledge of grassland dynamics, plant succession, and wildlife movement that I've seen among the graziers in my life. So I urge those who care about the meat industry's impact on the environment to bring more curiosity and humility to the discussion.

When we say "eat less meat" and end it there, we miss an opportunity to equip eaters with the means of sourcing protein that will not only nourish them but restore their home ecosystems. And behind every few hundred acres of land that goes poorly managed due to consumer miseducation is a land steward who can't do their work.

Appetite is energy. Rather than try to halt the tide of appetite for meat by discouraging its consumption outright, a better way to steward that energy would be to concentrate on where it can do the most good. In doing so, we're not just improving our environment, we're widening the demand for graziers who can produce meat and serve as ecological service providers.

So don't "eat less meat." Eat meat from people whose hands you can shake and whose ranches you can visit. Eat as much of that as you can afford, because that stuff comes from extensive production systems that impact hundreds and thousands of acres. Sourcing your protein from places you can account for means you can verify that their pastures are also habitat for foxes, badgers, burrowing owls, and bears—that you are keeping land wild and free. As I see it, beef raised in its environs beats a bean field any day as an ecologically just source of protein.

This type of meat isn't cheap—and you might find that you value it differently and stop taking it for granted. The end result may very well be that far less meat is consumed overall, at least for a while. But the quantity doesn't matter to me—what matters is what that animal did in its life on earth.

We have to pay for the world we want to live in. This means consuming the flesh of other sentient animals may damn well require a line-item on our budgets, alongside "eating out" and "entertainment." Maybe it's time we socialized ourselves and others to budget for environmental activism, and use that money to buy meat produced by the soil-building, grassland-loving graziers in our communities.

Viewpoint 2

> *"The ocean is home to vast mysteries, from the largest animal on the planet to microscopic organisms, which make up 98 per cent of the ocean's biomass. These microbes are essential to the food chain, the production of nutrients for land and sea, and the health of all animals and humans."*

All Life Depends on a Healthy Ocean

UN Environment Programme

This volume is about the rights of nonhuman animals, but sometimes our motivations for protecting other life is to protect ourselves. In this article, we learn how protecting the rights of sea-living animals helps to protect the lives of species that live on land—including human beings.

United Nations Environment Programme (2021). 5 reasons why a healthy ocean is linked to human rights. https://www.unep.org/news-and-stories/story/5-reasons-why-healthy-ocean-linked-human-rights [retrieved on 24 January 2025]. Reprinted by permission.

As you read, consider the following questions:

1. Why, according to this article, is the ocean so important to the human population?
2. How do healthy oceans fight the climate crisis?
3. How many species live in the ocean, according to this viewpoint?

We live on a blue planet, with oceans and seas covering more than 70 per cent of the Earth's surface. Oceans feed us, regulate our climate, and generate most of the oxygen we breathe.

But growing threats such as marine pollution, sea-level rising and over-fishing damage these aspects of our lives and infringe on the human rights attached to them. United Nations Environment Programme (UNEP) research shows, for example, that plastic pollution leakage into aquatic ecosystems has risen sharply in recent years and is projected to more than double by 2030.

In October 2021, the UN Human Rights Council recognized for the first time that a clean, healthy, and sustainable environment is a human right—a landmark move in the fight against the triple planetary crisis of climate change, nature and biodiversity loss and pollution and waste.

On this 10 December observance of Human Rights Day, the head of UNEP's Marine and Freshwater branch, Leticia Carvalho, outlines five reasons why a clean and healthy ocean is important for realizing human rights obligations relating to a clean, healthy, and sustainable environment.

The Ocean Is Our Life Support System

One-third of the total human population, nearly 2.4 billion people, live within 100 km (60 miles) of an oceanic coast—and all human life is dependent upon the oxygen and freshwater it creates.

Many societies—but not all—are able to take access to water, for drinking, sanitation and irrigation, for granted. In 2010, the

The Complexities of Culling: Balancing Ecosystems and Wildlife Management

Culling is the practice where individuals within an overpopulated species are killed based on selective characteristics such as age, genetic material, health, etc. This has now emerged as a form of conservation.

At its face value this may seem to be a very contradictory practice and at times I struggle with labeling this practice as a method of conservation but this concept has an extreme depth that is worth exploring. Of course this program specifically addresses those that are invasive species but also those whose populations have spiraled out of control, thus damaging the biodiversity and the ability for the ecosystem to stay balanced.

. . .

"Last year the federal threatened species scientific committee warned that feral horses could be "the crucial factor that causes final extinction" of six critically endangered animals and at least two critically endangered plants and said urgent action was necessary.

Under NSW law, the government must reduce the number of feral horses in the park to 3,000 by 2027 … the last population surveys in October, which estimated the number of feral horses in the park had ballooned to 17,000.

UN enshrined water as a human right. Without our ocean to power the planet's water cycle, and create fresh breathable air, we would not exist at all.

The Ocean Provides Food, Jobs and Livelihoods

The annual economic value of the ocean is estimated at USD $2.5 trillion, equivalent to the world's 7th largest economy. It provides nutrition, medicines, and mineral and renewable energy resources. It supports jobs in fishing, seafood, leisure and science.

> The Invasive Species Council's advocacy director, Jack Gough, said no one liked to see animals killed but the "sad reality" was a choice had to be made between urgently reducing the numbers of feral horses or accepting the destruction of sensitive alpine rivers, and the decline and extinction of native animals. The sad truth is that when an invasive species, or a species lacking a predator population, starts to take over it results in an unbalanced ecosystem. That species number skyrockets as they are able to reproduce and live unharmed and unaffected by predators. ... In the case of the feral horses this leads to overgrazing which progresses to habitat destruction. So not only are the horses eating food that other species need but they are also destroying tools of survival for other species such as areas where smaller species can hide or use for protection. This decreases the biodiversity and causes a chain reaction [so] that, if it goes unchecked, nothing will be able to be sustained there anymore. This is where the practice of culling comes into play.
>
> With any concept there are practical applications while also being abused in other situations. This is where intense regulation must be implemented to ensure that these practices are being carried out ethically with the intention that is best for the species and their ecosystem.
>
> **"The Complexities of Culling: Balancing Ecosystems and Wildlife Management" by Ross Park Zoo.**

Our ocean is the original "super-highway," that links economies together and transports goods and people all around the globe.

The Ocean Helps Fight the Climate Crisis

The ocean moderates the climate and influences our weather. Since the start of the industrial period, it has stored more than 90 per cent of the heat from human-caused climate change and one-third of the world's carbon emissions. Vital ecosystems such as mangroves, seagrasses and salt marshes could help us store more than 1.4bn tons of carbon emissions a year by 2050 if they are protected and restored.

The Ocean Is Home to Vast Biodiversity

According to the Convention on Biological Diversity, deep-seabed habitats alone host between 500,000 and 10 million species. But it is hard to know for sure, as some 80 per cent of the ocean remains unexplored and 91 per cent of marine species remain undescribed. What we do know is that we are continually making new discoveries.

In 2020, scientists discovered a detached 500-meter coral skyscraper, taller than the Empire State Building, off Australia's Great Barrier Reef. Precious and vulnerable coral reef ecosystems occupy less than 1 per cent of the ocean floor yet are home to at least 25 per cent of marine life. The ocean is home to vast mysteries, from the largest animal on the planet to microscopic organisms, which make up 98 per cent of the ocean's biomass. These microbes are essential to the food chain, the production of nutrients for land and sea, and the health of all animals and humans. In this Decade of Ocean Science, it is time to prioritize understanding and care for our ocean so that it can care for us.

The Ocean Provides Wellbeing Benefits to All Humanity

Most cultures on Earth have celebrated, valued, and sometimes feared the ocean. It has provided myths and legends, and inspiration for art, music and games. For example, UNEP is working with the videogame industry to raise ocean awareness.

In our leisure time, many of us enjoy beaches and activities such as swimming, surfing, sailing and diving, or simply the peace of mind that comes from being near water. The UN's Happiness Day recognizes happiness as a fundamental human goal. Like the rights to water, health, livelihoods and a clean environment, the ocean has a fundamental role to play.

Human Rights Day is observed every year on 10 December. The United Nations Environment Programme (UNEP) supports the recognition, advancement and implementation of human rights related to the environment in a multifaceted approach, including through the Environmental Rights Initiative - a package of rights-based work undertaken by UNEP and partners dedicated to promote, protect and respect human rights obligations relating to the enjoyment of a safe, clean, healthy and sustainable environment.

Viewpoint 3

> *"We might even start to think of nonhuman animals as fellow citizens. As citizens, animals could be entitled to workers' rights, health and retirement benefits."*

If Animals Had Rights, Things Might Not Change That Much

Steve Cooke

Elsewhere in this volume, many authors have argued that nonhuman animals should have rights. Some have said that some animals may not be sentient. However, this is the first viewpoint that actually explores what might happen if animals were given legal rights. Steve Cooke Associate Professor of Political Theory at the University of Leicester.

As you read, consider the following questions:

1. What are some of the places animals are used that most people don't know about, according to this viewpoint?
2. How would granting animal rights improve the environment, according to Cooke?
3. Cooke ends up by saying a world with animal rights might not be as hard to imagine as we might think. Do you agree?

Let's picture what our societies might look like if animals were granted rights against being killed, made to suffer or exploited for human gain.

When activists argue for animal rights, they ask us to imagine a different world. First, we need to understand how our lives are shaped by animals' lack of rights.

The range of uses we put animals to is enormous—going far beyond food, labour and clothing. We use gelatin to treat paper, from loo-roll to watercolour paper. Tallow finds its way into our banknotes, animal hair gives structure to suits and milk protein is found in condoms and any number of tablets. Beeswax and shellac (manufactured by crushing countless lac beetles) are used to make sweets shiny and treat wood. We even use waste from animal carcasses as biofuel.

Many religious and national festivals involve consuming meat or wearing costumes made from animal parts. Animal products are everywhere. We kill billions of animals to make them every year.

A call for animal rights is a call to forbid most of these uses in law. It is also a call to reconfigure our relationships with animals. Imagining such possibilities can be difficult. What's the point, we may wonder, of even considering the ethics of a future we can barely imagine?

One of the roles of philosophers working on animal ethics, I think, is to help us imagine. The humanities and social sciences try to answer the question "so how would that work?" That makes ethical possibilities, even unlikely ones, the subject of meaningful consideration.

The first thing to say is that although granting animals rights would dramatically change how we manufacture products, many of us may not even notice. Not only are vegan alternatives available for most animal products, but advances in technology make the use of animals possible without killing them or making them suffer. It is already possible to grow meat, eggs, milk, and leather in a lab without harming animals. In the future, scientific advances will probably make widescale production possible.

One change we might notice though, would be an improvement to our environment. Animal agriculture uses vast amounts of land, water and energy, both to house and feed animals, and pollutes our air, rivers and oceans.

One worry we might have is about the loss of jobs and income generated by animal agriculture. The sector is worth billions of pounds.

Animal rights theorists might respond in a number of ways: one would be to say that we ought not to protect jobs and income generated from rights violations. Another response might be to point to the fact that intensive animal agriculture largely depends on terrible working conditions, often suffered by marginalised groups of people.

Similarly, most of us probably wouldn't notice a ban on the use of animals in most forms of scientific research. New forms of animal-free modelling are now constantly being developed and many are well established. For example, advances in computer modelling allow scientists to predict how medicines will act in human patients without the need for testing on other animals.

Many people worry that we might not have achieved many of the medical advances we have without animal testing. This may well be true, but for animal rights advocates this isn't enough on its own to justify it.

A core purpose of a right is to protect the rights-bearer from being used as a means to benefit someone else. We can probably think of a great many deeply unethical practices that could benefit lots of people, but we rule them out because they would violate moral principles. In any case, if future advances are possible without harming nonhuman animals, then we ought to opt for alternative methods of research.

What about the uses we find for live animals, for example as workers, entertainers and companions? Even though many people love their pets as if they were family, there are some people who ask vets to have their pets killed because they no longer want them. Indeed, such cases are common enough that the veterinary profession has coined the term "convenience euthanasia". In these cases, vets do have the right to refuse to euthanise an animal. But there is ultimately no law to prevent vets from carrying out these instructions and many struggle with the ethics of doing so.

If companion animals had rights, then they would have to be treated differently. One possibility is that pets would become something much closer to a fostered family member. We might even start to think of nonhuman animals as fellow citizens. As citizens, animals could be entitled to workers' rights, health and retirement benefits.

When the police dog Finn was stabbed by a robbery suspect in 2016 in Stevenage, England, the judge trying the case found that all he could charge the defendant with was property damage.

Although Finn's case did result in the law being changed to prevent harm to service animals being justified as self-defence, it didn't substantially change the status of nonhuman animals in law.

Full animal rights mean that dogs like Finn would be entitled what is known as legal personhood. In some parts of the world, such as in the case of the river Magpie in Canada, there are already mechanisms like this for natural entities.

Once, people probably couldn't imagine a future where slavery was made illegal, or laughed at giving every adult in society a vote. I suspect that one day we will look back on the way we have treated nonhuman animals with a similar sense of disbelief.

When we try to imagine a world with animal rights, it turns out not to be so difficult after all. The concepts, technologies, and mechanisms needed are already in place, we just need to be brave enough to use them.

Viewpoint 4

> "In theory, we can use non-animal models for everything we use animal models for—and more."

We Won't Always Have to Use Animals for Medical Research

Greg Williams and Laura Anne Thomas

One area where it seems very difficult to respect animal rights is in medical research. However, the authors of this viewpoint discuss how it might soon be possible to conduct medical research without using any animals at all. Greg Williams is associate director at CSRIO Futures. CSIRO is Australia's national science agency. Laura Anne Thomas is the organization's strategy manager.

As you read, consider the following questions:

1. How have animals traditionally been used in medical research, according to this article?
2. What are organoids and organs on a chip?
3. How are non-animal models already being used in medical research?

Animals have been used for medical research for thousands of years, dating back to ancient Greece where the first dissections were performed.

These days, one of the main uses of animals is to ensure the safety of medical products before they're trialled in humans. But in addition to the important ethical reasons for minimising animal use, the reality is sometimes animals just aren't that good at predicting human responses. No animal model, for example, has captured all the human characteristics of complex illnesses like Alzheimer's disease or chronic inflammatory demyelinating polyneuropathy (a neuromuscular disease). This makes it hard to develop effective treatments and cures.

Thankfully, researchers are making progress in developing a collection of alternative approaches, called "non-animal models". A new report from our team at CSIRO Futures examines the potential of non-animal models and the actions Australia will need to take to pursue their use.

What Are Non-Animal Models?

Non-animal models are an alternative set of models that use human cells, tissues and data.

These have the potential to better mimic human responses. In doing so, this can more accurately predict if a medical product is likely to fail, allowing reinvestment in products that are more likely to succeed.

Computer simulations or "in silico models" are one example. These can be used across the medical product development process to complement—and in time potentially replace—other model types. They can be used in drug studies to model a drug's behaviour within the body, from cellular interactions to processes that involve multiple organs.

Complex three-dimensional biological models are also maturing quickly. Examples include:

- organoids—organ "buds" that can be propagated from stem cells or taken from biopsies
- organs-on-chips—cells cultured in a miniature engineered chip. These attempt to replicate the physical environment of human organs.

What Can We Use Non-Animal Models For?

In theory, we can use non-animal models for everything we use animal models for — and more. Simple non-animal models (human cells cultured over a flat surface) are already used to help identify drug targets due to their ability to test a large number of compounds and experimental conditions.

In the future, non-animal models will reduce—and eventually replace—animal use across a range of applications:

- screening potential drugs to see how well they work
- toxicology (safety) testing
- helping to screen, select and stratify shortlisted participants for clinical trials. This might include an assessment of their unique response to a potential drug.
- using patient cells to identify the treatment most likely to help that individual

Outside of medical products designed for humans, non-animal models can also support innovation in veterinary and agricultural medicines, cosmetic testing and eco-toxicology.

An Export Opportunity for Australia

Non-animal models present an economic opportunity for Australia, where the models, their components, and surrounding services could be exported to the world.

Our novel economic analysis sized the potential Australian market for two non-animal models: organoids and organs-on-chips. Other models were unable to be sized due to a lack of global market data. We estimate the Australian organoid market could be worth A$1.3 billion annually by 2040 and create 4,200 new jobs.

The organs-on-chips market could be worth A$300 million annually by 2040 and create 1,000 new jobs. This estimate is lower as this technology is currently less advanced but holds the potential to grow significantly beyond 2040.

Several Australian entities are already contributing to these opportunities. The Murdoch Children's Research Institute, for example, provides stem cell and modelling expertise as part of reNEW, a €300 million international collaboration.

Another example is from Schott Minifab, an international biotech and medical device company with Australian roots, which has successfully established scaled production of non-animal model components in Australia for domestic and export markets.

Making It a Reality

Non-animal models have already begun to complement and replace animal use in some areas, such as identifying drug targets. However, accelerating their development and adoption across a wider range of applications will require further technical advances to lower cost and validate their performance as superior models.

Australia has several research strengths in this field but we need a concentrated effort to help our research make it through to real world impact. Our report makes ten recommendations for supporting Australia's pursuit of these opportunities. Critical activities over the next five years include:

- coordinating local capabilities
- investing in upgraded infrastructure
- creating and collating data that compares animal and non-animal model performance.

Governments, industry and research must collaborate to deliver against these actions. Success will only come from collective efforts.

Periodical and Internet Sources Bibliography

The following articles have been selected to supplement the diverse views presented in this chapter.

Lena Beck, "What if Animals Had the Same Rights as Humans?" *Modern Farmer,* November 8, 2023. https://modernfarmer.com/2023/11/what-if-animals-had-the-same-rights-as-humans/.

CBS News, "Harvard study on monkeys reignites ethical debate over animal testing," CBS News, November 21, 2022. https://www.cbsnews.com/news/monkey-study-harvard-reignites-debate-animal-testing/

Christopher "Soul" Eubanks, "As a Black Man, I Felt Uncomfortable Becoming an Animal Activist," *Sentient*, March 1, 2021. https://sentientmedia.org/as-a-black-man-i-felt-uncomfortable-becoming-an-animal-activist/.

Nathan Heller, "If Animals Have Rights, Should Robots?" *New Yorker*, November 20, 2016.

Poorva Joshipura, "What do animal rights have to do with human wellbeing? Everything," *Down to Earth*, 5 September 2023. https://www.downtoearth.org.in/wildlife-biodiversity/what-do-animal-rights-have-to-do-with-human-wellbeing-everything-91583.

Douglas O. Linder, "The Case AGAINST Animal Personhood," *Famous Trials*. https://famous-trials.com/animalrights/2595-the-case-against-animal-personhood/

Emma Marris, "Modern Zoos Are Not Worth the Moral Cost," *New York Times*, June 11, 2021. https://www.nytimes.com/2021/06/11/opinion/zoos-animal-cruelty.html.

Julie Reardon, "Animal rights activists do not care about your animal's welfare," *Old Town Crier*, November 1, 2016. https://oldtowncrier.com/2016/11/01/animal-rights-activists-do-not-care-about-your-animals-welfare/.

Mikalah Singer and Aysha Akhtar, "With What Should We Replace Nonhuman Animals in Biomedical Research Protocols?" *American Medical Association Journal of Ethics*, September 2024. https://journalofethics.ama-assn.org/article/what-should-we-replace-nonhuman-animals-biomedical-research-protocols/2024-09.

Kristen Stilt, "Rights of Nature, Rights of Animals," *Harvard Law Review*, March 2021. https://harvardlawreview.org/forum/vol-134/rights-of-nature-rights-of-animals/.

For Further Discussion

Chapter 1

1. In the viewpoint that discusses how countries are ranked regarding their promotion of animal welfare, the author mentions the importance of cultural and religious attitudes. Do you think religion and culture affect how people treat animals in your country? If so, in what ways?
2. Were you surprised to learn, in viewpoint 3 of this chapter, that respect for animal welfare goes back thousands of years in many cultures? Can you think of reasons a culture might develop those attitudes? Why have many cultures lost their respect and concern for animals?
3. The UK's Sentience Act includes some invertebrates. Do you agree that animals such as lobsters, crab, and shrimp, perhaps even insects and spiders, might be sentient? What evidence would we need to determine that?

Chapter 2

1. In the second viewpoint in this chapter, philosopher Martha Nussbaum points out that we often judge an animal's value by how much that animal is like us. What is the problem with that way of thinking about animals? Where did that habit come from?
2. Several articles in this chapter pointed out that farm animals and animals that are grown for meat are generally not included in legislation that protects animals. Do you think these animals should have the same rights, if any, as wild animals and pets? Why or why not?
3. One of the authors in this chapter takes issue with research suggesting that fish can feel pain. His argument is that we can't prove that fish are conscious, and an animal must be conscious to suffer, even if it can respond to negative stimuli.

How would you define consciousness? What nonhuman animals do you think have it? What about humans?

Chapter 3

1. In the first viewpoint in this chapter, Jonathan Birch discusses how we have different feelings for animals that are further away from us evolutionarily, non-mammals, for the most part. Yet we are often repulsed by rodents. Birch refers to a famous study in which rats were taught to play the children's game hid-and-seek. Seeing those rats playing a familiar game with their human keepers changed a lot of people's minds about rats. Does the idea that rats can play hide-and-seek, and even giggle while playing, change your feelings about them?
2. India's Prevention of Cruelty to Animals Act defines "animal" as "any living creature other than a human being." That's certainly a reasonable definition, but can you see it being problematic in a legal sense? Could it lead to laws against, say, stepping on insects? What other examples can you think of?
3. In one viewpoint on this chapter, the author admitted that he greeted his teddy bear every day. In another, the author wrote that it is extremely difficult to prove scientifically that an animal is sentient. Do you think it would be better to err or on the side of caution and treat all animals as sentient, what we might call the "teddy bear approach"? Why or why not?

Chapter 4

1. The first viewpoint in this chapter is about how to best care for the environment that many animals depend on to survive. However, the solution, according to this author, involves eating animals. Contradictions like this occur often when considering the complicated issue of animal rights.

Can you think of other contradictory consequences of trying to protect all sentient species?

2. The ocean is home to tens of millions of species, most as yet undiscovered. Yet sea animals are rarely considered when discussing animals rights. Do you think that protecting oceans in general is a way of protecting animal rights?
3. In this chapter, Steve Cooke engages in a thought experiment about what the world might look like if animals had full rights. Can you do the same? What do you think the world would be like if animals were granted personhood?

Organizations to Contact

The editors have compiled the following list of organizations concerned with the issues debated in this book. The descriptions are derived from materials provided by the organizations. All have publications or information available for interested readers. The list was compiled on the date of publication of the present volume; the information provided here may change. Be aware that many organizations take several weeks or longer to respond to inquiries, so allow as much time as possible.

Alley Cat Allies

7920 Norfolk Avenue
Suite 600
Bethesda, MD 20814
240-482-1980
alleycat.org

Alley Cat Allies works in communities to champion low-cost spay and neuter policies and programs as well as lifesaving Trap-Neuter-Return (TNR) and Shelter-Neuter-Return (SNR).

American Society for the Prevention of Cruelty to Animals (ASPCA)

424 E. 92nd St
New York, NY 10128
212-876-7700
publicinformation@aspca.org
aspca.org

Founded in 1866, the ASPCA was the first animal welfare organization in North America. It works for legislative change that will protect the lives and welfare of animals.

Animal Welfare Institute

900 Pennsylvania Avenue, SE
Washington, DC 20003
202-337-2332
Contact via web form
awi@awionline.org

Since its founding in 1951, the Animal Welfare Institute has worked to alleviate animal suffering caused by humans. It seeks to improve the welfare of animals in agriculture, commerce, our homes and communities, in research, and in the wild.

Friends of Animals

777 Post Road
Suite 205
Darien, CT 06820
203-656-1522
Contact via website form
friendsofanimals.org

Since 1957, Friends of Animals has advocated for the rights of nonhuman animals, both free-living and domestic. Their goal is to free animals from cruelty and institutionalized exploitation around the world.

Humane World for Animals (formerly Humane Society of the United States/Humane Society International)

1255 23rd St. NW, Suite 450
Washington, DC 20037
202-452-1100 or 866-720-2676
Contact via web form
humaneworld.org

For more than 70 years, this organization has been a leader in the animal protection movement, working to address the root causes of animal cruelty and suffering in order to effect permanent change that will create a better world for animals.

Mercy for Animals

8033 Sunset Blvd, Suite 864,
Los Angeles, CA 90046
866-632-6446
Contact via web form
mercyforanimals.org

This organization focuses on ending factory farming. It envisions a world in which eating is an act of compassion and no one is exploited or forced to exploit another.

National Wildlife Federation

PO Box 1583, Merrifield, VA 22116-1583
800-822-9919
info@nwf.org
NWF.org

The NWF strives to protect ecosystems and improve the ecological balance in order to ensure safe, equitable access to clean water, air, and land to all wildlife and people.

Nonhuman Rights Project (NhRP)

611 Pennsylvania Avenue SE #345
Washington, DC 20003
Phone: 888-255-2612
info@nonhumanrights.org
nonhumanrights.org

The NhRP is the only civil rights organization in the United States dedicated solely to securing rights for nonhuman animals.

PETA—People for the Ethical Treatment of Animals

501 Front St., Norfolk, VA 23510
757-622-PETA (7382)
Contact via website form
peta.org

PETA is the largest animal liberation organization in the world, with more than 9 million members and supporters globally.

World Animal Protection

126 Fairlie Road, Slough, SL1 4PY, UK
44 (0)20 7239 0500
info@worldanimalprotection.org
worldanimalprotection.org

World Animal Protection is dedicated to ending animal cruelty and suffering worldwide.

Bibliography of Books

Jonathan Birch. *The Edge of Sentience: Risk and Precaution in Humans, Other Animals, and AI*. Oxford, UK: Oxford University Press, 2024.

George Bumann. *Eavesdropping on Animals: What We Can Learn From Wildlife Conversations*. Vancouver, BC: Greystone Press, 2024.

Raffael N. Fasel and Sean C. Butler. *Animal Rights Law*. Oxford, UK: Hart, 2023.

Gary Francione. *Why Veganism Matters: The Moral Value of Animals*. New York, NY: Columbia University Press, 2020.

Ernest Freeberg. *A Traitor to His Species: Henry Bergh and the Birth of the Animal Rights Movement*. New York, NY: Basic, 2020.

Leah Garcés. *Transfarmation: The Movement to Free Us from Factory Farming*. Boston, MA: Beacon Press, 2024.

Peter Godfrey-Smith. *Metazoa: Animal Minds and the Birth of Consciousness*. New York, NY: HarperCollins, 2021.

Rick McIntyre. *Thinking Like a Wolf: Lessons From the Yellowstone Packs*. Vancouver, BC: Greystone Press, 2024.

Brittany Michelson and Ingrid Newkirk. *Voices for Animal Liberation: Inspirational Accounts by Animal Rights Activists*. New York, NY: Skyhorse, 2020.

Sy Montgomery. And Warren K. Carlyle IV. *Secrets of the Octopus*. Washington, DC: National Geographic Books.

Martha C. Nussbaum. *Justice for Animals: Our Collective Responsibility*. New York, NY: Simon and Schuster, 2024.

Mark Rowlands. *Animal Rights*. Cambridge, MA: MIT Press, 2025.

Jeff Sebo. *The Moral Circle: Who Matters, What Matters, and Why*. New York, NY: Norton, 2025.

Peter Singer. *Animal Liberation Now: The Definitive Classic Renewed*. New York, NY: Diversion Books (Harper Collins), 2024.

Marianne Taylor. *The Animal Mind: Profiles of Intelligence and Emotion*. New York, NY; Abrams, 2024.

Bill Wasik and Monica Murphy. *Our Kindred Creatures: How Americans Came to Feel the Way They Do About Animals*. New York, NY: Alfred A. Knopf, 2024.

Ed Yong. *An Immense World: How Animal Senses Reveal the Hidden Realms Around Us*. New York. NY; Random House, 2023.

Index

E

F

G

H

I

J

L

M

N

O

P

R

S

T

V

W

Z